FOUNDATIONS OF
ECUMENICAL SOCIAL THOUGHT

FOUNDATIONS OF ECUMENICAL SOCIAL THOUGHT

THE OXFORD CONFERENCE REPORT

Report of the
Conference on Church, Community and State
at Oxford, July 12-25, 1937

edited by
J. H. OLDHAM

with an Introduction by
HAROLD L. LUNGER

FORTRESS PRESS   PHILADELPHIA

CONTENTS

INTRODUCTION

T HE OXFORD CONFERENCE of 1937 remains today a
landmark in ecumenical social thinking." This
judgment of the Department on Church and Society of the
World Council of Churches in 1956 will be concurred in
by all those acquainted with the subject. So will the
further assertion that anyone "who wants to understand
the roots of modern ecumenical social thinking must
eventually go back to the documents of Oxford for guidance. . . . [For] Oxford, more than any other one event in
the history of the ecumenical movement, set the compass
for the course which the churches were to follow in their
work in this field."[1]

The positions on social issues taken by the Amsterdam,
Evanston, and New Delhi assemblies, together with the
actions of the Central Committee and other groups within
the World Council of Churches, often become considerably clearer when seen in the light of Oxford. Moreover,
as churchmen prepare for the forthcoming World Conference on Church and Society in 1966—the first ecumenical conference in twenty-nine years to be devoted
exclusively to the concerns of Christian Life and Work—
it will be especially important that they review the findings of Oxford.

The reports of the Oxford Conference, however, have
more than historical importance. John C. Bennett, writ-
ing in 1954, stated that this conference "is considered by

---

[1] World Council of Churches, Division of Studies, Department of Church
and Society, *Statements of the World Council of Churches on Social Questions: With a Preface on the Development of Ecumenical Social Thinking*
(2nd ed.; Geneva: World Council of Churches, 1956), pp. 7–8.

many Protestants to have produced the most significant body of Christian social teachings in the modern period."[2] In 1963 Walter Muelder referred to Oxford as being "to date the high water mark in ecumenical ethics."[3] Textbooks in Christian ethics and books dealing with a variety of contemporary social issues continue to make use of the insights of the Oxford Conference.

Unfortunately, it had become increasingly difficult to gain access to these important documents, since the official report of this conference, edited by J. H. Oldham, has been long out of print. This new edition makes them available once again.

Oxford, the second of the great ecumenical conferences to be devoted to the social tasks of the church, was convened by the Universal Christian Council on Life and Work just before it merged with the Faith and Order Movement to form the World Council of Churches.

The first Life and Work Conference at Stockholm in 1925 represented the convergence of the social gospel movement and the peace movement. Stockholm was fed by four major tributaries: the Federal Council of the Churches of Christ in America, at once the child of and the leading organizational arm of the social concern of American Protestantism; the World Alliance for Promoting International Friendship through the Churches, founded upon the passionate but frustrated efforts of Christian leaders in many countries to keep the peace prior to 1914 and to re-establish it in the years immediately following; the Conference of Christian Politics, Economics and Citizenship, held in Birmingham in 1924, one of the

---

[2] John C. Bennett et al., *Christian Values and Economic Life* ("Series on Ethics and Economic Life"; New York: Harper, 1954), p. 227.

[3] Walter G. Muelder, "Building a Basic Theological Library—X: Christian Social Ethics Bookshelf," *The Christian Century*, 70, No. 44 (October 30, 1963), 1337.

significant expressions of the British Christian social movement; and the Church of Sweden which, prompted by
Archbishop Söderblom, initiated numerous efforts to make
the churches a reconciling force among the nations.

While Stockholm produced no extensive findings or
reports, it did mark the beginning of ecumenical thinking
on social issues.[4] It focused attention of the churches
upon their tasks in society and brought together many of
those whose common concerns, growing friendship, mutual trust, and cross-fertilization of thought were to
provide the basis for the epoch-making achievements of
Oxford twelve years later. The Continuation Committee
set up at Stockholm was reconstituted in 1930 as a permanent body—the Universal Christian Council for Life and
Work.

In the years following Stockholm further research
studies were carried on and smaller conferences held.
Considerable attention was directed to the theological
foundations of Christian social action as well as to other
more concrete issues as they emerged.

In the meantime a worldwide depression and consequent large-scale unemployment presented an urgent
challenge to the Christian conscience, military action in
Manchuria and Spain posed a new threat to world peace,
and the rise of totalitarianism in Italy and more especially
in Germany raised a whole series of problems concerning
the nature of the church and its relation to the secular
community and state.

In 1934 the decision was made to hold another ecumenical conference—on the theme "Church, Community and
State." The aim of the conference was not merely to

[4] See *The Stockholm Conference, 1925: The Official Report of the Universal Christian Conference on Life and Work Held in Stockholm, 19-30
August, 1925*, ed. G. K. A. Bell (London: Oxford University Press, 1926).

redefine in traditional terms the relative roles of "two parallel and complementary societies which respectively order and guide the temporal and spiritual life of the community."[5]   It was rather to consider the issues posed by the rise of the totalitarian state, the problem of "how religion is to survive in a single community which is neither church nor state, which recognizes no formal limits, but which covers the whole of life and claims to be the source and goal of every human activity."[6]   In the words of the editor of the Oxford Conference report, "The essential theme of the Oxford Conference, as was stated in the first announcement of it, was the life-and-death struggle between Christian faith and the secular and pagan tendencies of our time."[7]

The Research Department of the Universal Christian Council for Life and Work immediately launched an amazingly ambitious program of research in preparation for the conference scheduled for 1937.   Outstanding scholars and churchmen from major Protestant and Orthodox bodies were drawn into the enterprise.   More than a dozen small international consultations were held for preliminary study of problems to come before the conference, and a continuous interchange of thought was carried on through the preparation and circulation of more than a hundred study papers.   Written in the first place by some of Christendom's outstanding scholars, these papers were submitted to numerous others for criticism and comment.   As the process went on, the documents were revised and rewritten—some of them several times.

[5] Christopher Dawson, as cited by J. H. Oldham (ed.), *The Oxford Conference (Official Report)* (Chicago: Willett, Clark & Co., 1937), p. 1.   British edition published under the title *The Churches Survey Their Task: The Report of the Conference at Oxford, July 1937, On Church, Community and State* (London: George Allen & Unwin, 1937).

[6] Dawson, *ibid.*

[7] *Ibid.*, p. 2.

Out of these studies came six volumes, published shortly after Oxford, dealing with many acute issues of social concern and bearing the titles *The Christian Understanding of Man; The Kingdom of God and History; Christian Faith and the Common Life; Church and Community; Church, Community and State in Relation to Education;* and *The Universal Church and the World of Nations.*[8] The list of contributors to these volumes reads like a "Who's Who" of twentieth-century Christian scholarship. Included are names like Calhoun, Brunner, Maury, Horton, Dodd, Bevan, Dawson, Tillich, Dibelius, Niebuhr, Temple, Farmer, Latourette, Bennett, Boegner, Lilje, Dulles, Piper, and Raven. In addition, important preparatory studies were written by J. H. Oldham and W. A. Visser 't Hooft on *The Church and Its Function in Society*[9] and Nils Ehrenström on *Christian Faith and the Modern State: An Ecumenical Approach.*[10]

Against the background of these extensive advance preparations, 425 delegates assembled in Oxford on July 12, 1937, for a two-week conference. One hundred and twenty religious bodies in forty countries had appointed official delegates. Approximately one hundred of the conference members were laymen representing a wide variety of vocational interests and areas of technical competence. Three hundred of the participants were from the United States of America and the British Commonwealth, forty represented the Eastern and Orthodox bodies, and thirty the so-called younger churches. While the conference was widely representative, two bodies were

[8] All volumes published in Chicago by Willett, Clark & Co., 1938; in London by George Allen & Unwin, 1938.

[9] Chicago: Willett, Clark & Co., 1937; London: George Allen & Unwin, 1937.

[10] Trans. Denzil Patrick and Olive Wyon (Chicago: Willett, Clark & Co., 1937; London: SCM Press, 1937).

conspicuously absent: the Roman Catholic Church and the German Evangelical Church, the former by its own choice, the latter because of restrictions by the German government.[11]

The agenda provided a number of deeply moving experiences of common worship, including a thread of daily morning and evening prayers. During the first week a dozen penetrating addresses were given by leaders of the world church.

[11] Though the question proved quite academic in the end, considerable discussion took place in the years leading up to Oxford concerning who should represent the Evangelical Christians of Germany at the conference. As early as June, 1934, Dietrich Bonhoeffer wrote Bishop G. K. A. Bell, chairman of the Universal Christian Council for Life and Work, asking whether the *Reichskirche* had not in fact "ceased to be a Christian church at all," by virtue of its acceptance of the "Aryan paragraph" (requiring the exclusion from the church of all Christians of Jewish descent), its demand for unreserved homage to the state, its use of force and prohibition of free elections, and its giving of autocratic powers to Bishop Müller, head of the *Reichskirche*. (See the exchange of letters between Bonhoeffer and Bell dated June 29, 1934, in Edwin H. Robertson [ed.], *No Rusty Swords* [New York: Harper, 1965], pp. 273–77.) To the suggestion that the Confessing Church constitute itself a "free church" and petition for recognition at Oxford alongside the *Reichskirche*, Bonhoeffer replied that the Confessing Church claimed to be "the only theologically and legally legitimate Evangelical Church in Germany" (*ibid.*, p. 283). Given the constitution and structure of the Universal Christian Council, however, the council's leaders felt it impossible to exclude the *Reichskirche* in favor of the Confessing Church. Both churches took part in the preparations for Oxford. When the delegates of the Confessing Church applied for their passports to the conference, however, they were unable to secure them. Indeed by this time some of them were either in prison or special custody or under close surveillance. The German government also decided against allowing delegates of the *Reichskirche* to come to Oxford. In view of the forced absence of all official German delegates, the conference issued a special message expressing brotherly concern for the trials being suffered by both Evangelical and Roman Catholic Christians in Germany. It also expressed a special sense of solidarity and sympathy for members of the Confessing Church who "have stood firm from the first in the Confessional church for the sovereignty of Christ, and for the freedom of the church of Christ to preach his gospel" (J. H. Oldham, *The Oxford Conference*, Appendix A, p. 259).

The conference, however, had been assembled not to listen to speeches, but to clarify and crystallize Christian thought and strategy in regard to the burning issues of human society. This work was done largely in the five sections, each with about eighty members and its own assigned topic. During the first week these met simultaneously for four full mornings and three or four evenings.

In addition to the preparatory studies already referred to, each section had in its hands a draft report prepared in advance for its use. In most cases these were laid aside after preliminary discussion, and the delegates set out to prepare documents of their own which would better express the thinking of the section members. The reports which emerged from this process thus represent not the conclusions of a few individuals but the result of genuine group thinking. In two cases the original draft reports were also revised by the sections and included in the official report as "additional reports."

During the second week the section reports were carefully considered by the conference as a whole, two sessions being given to the discussion of each. They were then recommitted to the sections for further revision in light of the plenary discussions. No attempt was made to approve the reports in detail. Without acting upon the final revisions, the conference "commended" the reports "to the serious and favorable consideration of the churches."

In addition, the conference drafted and approved a "Message" containing a brief summary of the major concerns dealt with in more detail in the reports themselves. This makes a convenient introduction to the documents of the conference.

The original editor of the reports points out that "it was not the aim of the conference to issue authoritative pronouncements. . . . Its object was to provide . . . as comprehensive and balanced a statement as was possible, in the time and with the resources at its disposal, of the present mind of the church."[12] In other words, the reports did not seek to be "prophetic," pointing out the direction in which Christian thinking *ought* to move, but rather to set forth the actual beliefs of the delegates. When, as in the case of Christian participation in warfare, there was no agreement, this was frankly recognized and the divergent views were set forth as clearly and forthrightly as possible.

Nevertheless the reports demonstrate a large consensus of Christian thought and judgment. They are significant because "what they say is what a large body of Christians, representatives of diverse countries and Christian traditions, were prepared—on the whole, and doubtless with many qualifications on specific points on the part of individual members of the conference—to say *together*."[13]

This, indeed, is what makes the Oxford Conference reports so significant and gives them the only kind of "authority" that any Protestant ecumenical statement can have. It is in this sense that a competent historian can declare that "the authority of the Oxford reports was unprecedented, at least in Protestant social ethics."[14]

Not only did Oxford leave a valuable deposit in the formal reports it issued, but it also pioneered in patterns of ecumenical study and discussion which have been followed in large part ever since: careful advance study and research, thorough discussion in smaller groups, drafting of reports, their discussion in plenary session and sub-

12 J. H. Oldham, *The Oxford Conference*, p. 16.
13 *Ibid.*, pp. 16–17.
14 J. H. Nichols, *Democracy and the Churches* (Philadelphia: Westminster Press, 1951), p. 235.

sequent revision, and finally the commending of the reports to the churches for further study and action. This is substantially the pattern followed by the World Council today in its conferences and assemblies, and by the various study conferences convened by the Federal and then the National Council of the Churches of Christ in the United States of America.

What follows in this volume are the Message and the section reports taken verbatim from the official report edited by J. H. Oldham. The forty-five page introduction has been omitted, along with the appendices giving the conference program, names of officers and delegates, and certain official actions of the conference.[15]

A definitive account of the development of the Life and Work Movement from its beginnings at Stockholm through Oxford may be found in the chapter by Nils Ehrenström, "Movements for International Friendship and Life and Work, 1925-1948," in *A History of the Ecumenical Movement, 1517-1948,* edited by Ruth Rouse and Stephen C. Neill.[16]

Harold L. Lunger

Brite Divinity School
Texas Christian University
Fort Worth, Texas
October, 1965

[15] Since the body of this edition has been reproduced photographically with only the page numbers changed, the student who wishes to look up references based on the original edition may do so by subtracting 44 from the page reference given. That is to say, a reference to page 60 in the original edition will be found on page 16 in this edition.

[16] London: SPCK, 1954, pp. 545-596.

A MESSAGE FROM THE OXFORD CONFERENCE TO THE CHRISTIAN CHURCHES

THE DELEGATES to the World Conference on Church, Community and State, assembled at Oxford from July 12 to 26, 1937, send at the close of their deliberations the following message to the Churches of Christ throughout the world: —

In the name of Christ, greetings.

We meet at a time when mankind is oppressed with perplexity and fear. Men are burdened with evils almost insupportable and with problems apparently insoluble. Even in countries which are at peace unemployment and malnutrition sap men's strength of body, mind and spirit. In other countries war does its " devil's work," and threatens to overwhelm us all in its limitless catastrophe.

Yet we do not take up our task as bewildered citizens of our several nations, asking if anywhere there is a clue to our problems; we take it up as Christians, to whom is committed " the word of reconciliation," that " God was in Christ reconciling the world unto himself."

The first duty of the church, and its greatest service to the world, is that it be in very deed the church — confessing the true faith, committed to the fulfillment of the will of Christ, its only Lord, and united in him in a fellowship of love and service.

We do not call the world to be like ourselves, for we are already too like the world. Only as we ourselves repent, both as individuals and as corporate bodies, can the church call men to repentance. The call to ourselves and to the world is to Christ.

Despite our unfaithfulness God has done great things through his church. One of the greatest is this, that, notwithstanding the tragedy of our divisions and our inability in many important matters to speak with a united voice, there exists an actual world-fellowship. Our unity in Christ is not a theme for aspiration; it is an experienced fact. We can speak of it with boldness because our conference is an illustration of it. We are drawn from many nations and from many different communions, from churches with centuries of history behind them and from the younger churches whose story covers but a few decades; but we are one in Christ.

The unity of this fellowship is not built up from its constituent parts, like a federation of different states. It consists in the sovereignty and redeeming acts of its one Lord. The source of unity is not the consenting movement of men's wills; it is Jesus Christ whose one life flows through the body and subdues the many wills to his.

The Christian sees distinctions of race as part of God's purpose to enrich mankind with a diversity of gifts. Against racial pride or race antagonism the church must set its face implacably as rebellion against God. Especially in its own life and worship there can be no place for barriers because of race or color. Similarly the Christian accepts national communities as part of God's purpose to enrich and diversify human life. Every man is called of God to serve his fellows in the community to which he belongs. But national egotism tending to the suppression of other nationalities or of minorities is, no less than individual egotism, a sin against the Creator of all peoples and races. The deification of nation, race or class, or of political or cultural ideals, is idolatry, and can lead only to increasing division and disaster.

On every side we see men seeking for a life of fellowship

in which they experience their dependence on one another. But because community is sought on a wrong basis, the intensity of the search for it issues in conflict and disintegration. In such a world the church is called to be in its own life that fellowship which binds men together in their common dependence on God and overleaps all barriers of social status, race or nationality.

In consonance with its nature as true community, the church will call the nations to order their lives as members of the one family of God. The universal church, surveying the nations of the world, in every one of which it is now planted and rooted, must pronounce a condemnation of war unqualified and unrestricted. War can occur only as a fruit and manifestation of sin. This truth is unaffected by any question of what may be the duty of a nation which has to choose between entry upon war and a course which it believes to be a betrayal of right, or what may be the duty of a Christian citizen whose country is involved in war. The condemnation of war stands, and also the obligation to seek the way of freeing mankind from its physical, moral and spiritual ravages. If war breaks out, then preeminently the church must manifestly be the church, still united as the one body of Christ, though the nations wherein it is planted fight one another, consciously offering the same prayers that God's name may be hallowed, his kingdom come, and his will be done in both, or all, the warring nations. This fellowship of prayer must at all costs remain unbroken. The church must also hold together in one spiritual fellowship those of its members who take different views concerning their duty as Christian citizens in time of war.

To condemn war is not enough. Many situations conceal the fact of conflict under the guise of outward peace. Christians must do all in their power to promote among the nations justice and peaceful cooperation, and the means of peaceful adjustment to altering conditions. Especially should Christians in more fortunate countries press the demand for justice on behalf of the less fortunate. The insistence upon justice must express itself in a demand for such mitigation of the sovereignty of national states as is involved in the abandonment by each of the claim to be judge in its own cause.

We recognize the state as being in its own sphere the highest authority. It has the God-given aim in that sphere to uphold law and order and to minister to the life of its people. But as all authority is from God, the state stands under his judgment. God is himself the source of justice, of which the state is not lord but servant. The Christian can acknowledge no ultimate authority but God; his loyalty to the state is part of his loyalty to God and must never usurp the place of that primary and only absolute loyalty.

The church has duties laid upon it by God which at all cost it must perform, among which the chief is to proclaim the word of God and to make disciples, and to order its own life in the power of the Spirit dwelling in it. Because this is its duty it must do it, whether or not the state consents; and the state on its side should recognize the duty and assure full liberty for its performance. The church can claim such liberty for itself only as it is also concerned for the rights and liberties of others.

In the economic sphere the first duty of the church is to insist that economic activities, like every other department of human life, stand under the judgment of Christ. The existence of economic classes presents a barrier to human fellowship which cannot be tolerated by the Christian conscience. Indefensible inequalities of opportunity in regard to education, leisure and health continue to prevail. The ordering of economic life has tended to enhance acquisitiveness and to set up a false standard of economic and social success. The only forms of employment open to many men and women, or the fact that none is open, prevent them from finding a sense of Christian vocation in their daily life.

We are witnessing new movements which have arisen in reaction to these evils but which combine with their struggle for social justice the repudiation of all religious faith. Aware of the reality of sin, the church knows that no change in the outward ordering of life can of itself eradicate social evil. The church therefore cannot surrender to the utopian expectations of these movements, and their godlessness it must unequivocally reject; but in doing so it must recognize that Christians in their blindness to the challenging evils of the economic order have been partly responsible for the antireligious character of these movements.

Christians have a double duty — both to bear witness to their faith within the existing economic order and also to test all economic institutions in the light of their understanding of God's will. The forces of evil against which Christians have to contend are found not only in the hearts of men as individuals, but have entered into and infected the structure of society, and there also must be combated. The responsibility of the church is to insist on the true relationship of spiritual and economic goods. Man cannot live without bread, and man cannot live by bread alone. Our human wealth consists in fellowship with God and in him with our brethren. To this fellowship the whole economic order must be made subservient.

The questions which have mainly engaged the attention of the conference are questions that can be effectively dealt with, in practice, only by the laity. Those who are responsible for the daily conduct of industry, administration and public life must discover for themselves what is the right decision in an endless variety of concrete situations. If they are to receive the help they need in making responsible Christian decisions new types of ministry will have to be developed by the church.

The fulfillment of the tasks to which the church is called today lies largely in the hands of youth. Many loud voices are calling on young people to give themselves to political and social ideals, and it is often hard for them to hear the voice of Jesus Christ who calls them to be servants of the eternal kingdom. Yet many of the younger generation, often in spite of ridicule and sometimes of persecution, are turning to him, and individually as well as in Christian youth movements devote themselves to the renewal of the life of the churches and to making known the good news of Christ by word and action. We rejoice in their brave witness.

In the education of youth the church has a twofold task. First, it must be eager to secure for every citizen the fullest possible opportunity for the development of the gifts that God has bestowed on him. In particular, the church must condemn inequality of educational opportunity as a main obstacle to fullness of fellowship in the life of the community.

While the church is thus concerned with all education it has, also, a special responsibility to realize its own understanding of the meaning and end of education in the relation of life to God. In education, as elsewhere, if God is not recognized he is ignored. The church must claim the liberty to give a Christian education to its own children. It is in the field of education that the conflict between Christian faith and non-Christian conceptions of the ends of life, between the church and an all-embracing community life which claims to be the source and goal of every human activity, is in many parts of the world most acute. In this conflict all is at stake, and the church must gird itself for the struggle.

As we look to the future it is our hope and prayer that the Spirit of God may cause new life to break forth spontaneously in a multitude of different centers, and that there may come into being a large number of " cells " of Christian men and women associated in small groups for the discovery of fresh ways in which they may serve God and their fellow men.

We have deeply felt the absence from our fellowship of the churches that have not been represented at the conference. Our hearts are filled with anguish as we remember the suffering of the church in Russia. Our sympathy and gratitude go out to our Christian brethren in Germany; we are moved to a more living trust by their steadfast witness to Christ and we pray that we may be given grace to bear the same clear witness to the Lord.

We have much to encourage us since the conference at Stockholm twelve years ago. The sense of the unity of the church in all the world grows stronger every year. We trust that this cause will be yet more fully served by the world council of churches, proposals for which have been considered by the conference and commended to the churches.

We have tried during these days at Oxford to look without illusion at the chaos and disintegration of the world, the injustices of the social order and the menace and horror of war. The world is anxious and bewildered and full of pain and fear. We are troubled, yet we do not despair. Our hope is anchored in the living God. In Christ, and in the union of man with God and of man with man, which he creates, life even in face of all these evils has a meaning.

In his name we set our hands as the servants of God, and in him of one another, to the task of proclaiming God's message of redemption, of living as his children and of combating injustice, cruelty and hate. The church can be of good cheer; it hears its Lord saying, " I have overcome the world."

THE REPORTS OF THE SECTIONS OF THE CONFERENCE

I. REPORT OF THE SECTION ON CHURCH AND COMMUNITY *

1. THE WORLD TODAY

THE CHRISTIAN church is called upon to fulfill its mission today amid a distraught and disunited mankind. Divisions and conflicts there have always been, but the foundations of communal life in generally accepted systems of customs, social distinctions, moral and cultural values and religious beliefs have remained sufficiently firm to preserve the essential structure of the various communities in which men have lived their lives together. Today, however, as probably only once or twice before in human history, the foundations themselves are shaken. Traditional pieties and loyalties and standards of conduct have lost their unquestioned authority; no new ones have taken their place. As a result, the community life of mankind has been thrown into confusion and disintegration. Though more marked in some sections of mankind than in others these facts are in some measure universal. This social disunity is reflected in the life of the individual man or woman, whose personal destiny is largely bound up with his relation to the community. When society " goes to pieces " the individual tends also to " go to pieces " in suffering, frustration and a baffled sense of the futility and meaninglessness of his existence.

* The report, after receiving the approval of the section, was submitted to the conference substantially in its present form. The conference received the report, referred it back to the section for revision in the light of the discussion and commended it to the serious and favorable consideration of the churches. The report was revised by the section and approved by it in its present form.

In many countries vigorous attempts are being made to restore social unity by drastic control and regimentation and by making national or class unity the supreme good to take precedence of all else. These attempts bear witness to the truth of what has just been said and to the primal need of human life as God has made it for community and fellowship.

In the midst of such a world, torn and disrupted and feverishly seeking a way out of its troubles, the church of Jesus Christ has to preach its message and fulfill its task. What is it to say? How is it to act? What are individual Christians to believe and to do?

2. THE CALL TO THE CHURCH

The church is under obligation to proclaim the truth that the disintegration of society has one root cause. Human life is falling to pieces because it has tried to organize itself into unity on a secularistic and humanistic basis without any reference to the divine will and power above and beyond itself. It has sought to be self-sufficient, a law unto itself. Nor is there any hope in the ascription of sacred quality to nation or state or class. A false sacred, a false God, merely adds demonic power to the unredeemed passions of men. Though bringing about temporary and local unity it prepares for mankind an even worse and wider conflict. The recall to God in penitence must stand first.

Yet how shall men know who and what God is, and what it is of which they must repent, and in what new direction they must walk, and whence they may find strength to walk therein? The answer to these questions God himself has given in the revelation of his will and supremely in Jesus Christ. In God is the secret of true unity among men and in Christ is revealed the secret of God. The first task of the church, now as always, is to make known the gospel, and to assert the claim of Jesus Christ as the incarnate Word of God to the lordship of all human life.

The modern world, however, has never been wholly without the preaching of the gospel. Dare we ascribe its present plight solely to its willful rejection of the word of life and of the things which belong to its peace? Nay, is not the modern situation God's call to a church[1] which has been content to preach the redeeming word without the costly redeeming deed? Has it taken the trouble to make plain to itself or to the world the meaning of its redeeming word for the daily life of mankind? What reason has the church given the world to believe that it possesses the secret of true community in him whom it preaches and whom it professes to serve? The life of the church is deeply infected with the very ills from which humanity suffers. The divisions and the conflicts of mankind have been reproduced and even justified within its own borders. Again and again Christian groups have persecuted and sought to destroy one another and with equal guilt have persecuted men of other faiths, and this is still happening today. The church's recall of the world to the feet of Christ must be preceded by the recall of itself. The church is under call to confess its sin and to seek anew from God forgiveness and the cleansing of its life.

But there is peril in these general propositions, true as they may be. The call to Christians to repent and submit their lives anew to God in Christ has to be obeyed in the midst of the concrete realities of the common life, where decisions have to be taken and acts with all their irrevocable consequences done. Perplexities and problems at once arise. They press the more heavily the more earnestly the

[1] In this document, where the church as an institution is referred to organized Christianity and not the *una sancta* is meant.

Christian believer seeks to bring everything in his life into the obedience of Christ.

The difficulties arise in the main because the Christian finds himself called upon at every point to act in relation to systems or frameworks of life which partake of both good and evil; they are of God and yet also of human sin. The orders of family, community, people, nation, are part of the God-given basis and structure of human life without which the individual would have no existence at all; yet man's sin — his pride, greed, fear, idolatry — has infected them all. Hence the Christian who has seen the perfect will of God in Christ and would serve that will in the midst of his fellow men finds himself in perpetual tension and conflict. He accepts thankfully his community in order to live and to work in it and for it; yet if he would work in it and for it for Christ he must be in continuous protest against it.

The difficulty of deciding how far in particular instances the Christian should go in cooperation with ways of life which are in greater or less degree contrary to God's will is often great, and the danger of self-deception is always present. No general principle of guidance can be laid down. That the ways of the community or nation may reach such a pitch of evil that there is no option for the church but to repudiate them altogether, and even at times refuse cooperation with them, can hardly be questioned in view of contemporary events; but just where that point is must be left to the guidance of the Spirit. This, however, must be said: The church is under obligation never to lose sight of its one supreme calling to bear costing witness, in deed as well as in word, to the higher way of life in Christ. Where it must join in what it feels to be a partial approach to the perfect will of Christ, it must keep its spirit sensitive and humble by continual acknowledgment before God of the sin of mankind which is wresting the gifts of God to evil ends, and in which it is itself implicated. This is the tragic and continuous tension in which the church is always placed, the tension between the pure ideals of the kingdom and the unredeemed community of men in which it has to live and bear its witness. But so soon as it seeks peace by becoming unconscious of that tension then it is traitorous to its Master and Lord.

Three problems in the church's relation to the community today urgently demand attention.

(a) *The Church and the National Community (Volk)*. The church comes to men never as isolated individuals. Every man is born into a specific national community and is united to it by strong ties. The church regards this fact of nationality, in spite of its infection by human sinfulness, as essentially a gift of God to mankind.

The love of the Christian for his people should therefore be part of his gratitude to God for the riches which are his through the community into which he has been born. The primary call on the loyalty and service, both of the church and of the individual Christian believer, will be, as a rule, the community in which God has set him. Every church should regard itself as a church for the whole people. This means that it accepts its place in the community life and acknowledges its responsibility, along with all other Christian bodies, to reach all members of the community, in relation to every aspect of their life, with the pure message of the gospel. It does not mean that it subordinates itself to the national life.

As with every divine gift, the gift of national community has been and is being abused by men and made to serve sin. Any form of national egotism whereby the love of one's own people leads to the suppression of other nationalities or national minorities, or to the failure to respect and appreciate the gifts of other people, is sin and rebellion against God, who is the Creator and Lord of all peoples. Even more, to see in one's own nation the source and standard of saving revelation, or in any way to give the nation divine status, is sin. This is to be utterly repudiated and irreconcilably opposed by the Christian conscience in the name of God and for the sake of the nation it is called to serve. Further, the church is called to be watchful that these evils, or the world views by which they are supported, do not enter within its own life, destroying its fellowship and corrupting the pure word of the gospel of Jesus Christ which has been entrusted to it.[2]

(b) *The Church and Race.* Even deeper are distinctions of race. The existence of black races, white races, yellow races, is to be accepted gladly and reverently as full of possibilities under God's purpose for the enrichment of human life. And there is no room for any differentiation between the races as to their intrinsic value. All share alike in the concern of God, being created by him to bring their unique and distinctive contributions to his service in the world.

Here again, however, the gift can be and is abused. The sin of man asserts itself in racial pride, racial hatreds and persecutions and in the exploitation of other races. Against this attitude in all its forms the church is called by God to set its face implacably and to utter its word unequivocally both within and without its own borders.

Moreover, it is a first responsibility of the church to demonstrate within its own fellowship the reality of community as God intends it. It is commissioned to call all men into the church, into a divine society that transcends all national and racial limitations and divisions. In the services of wor-

[2] In view of the immediate urgency of this problem a supplementary declaration is appended at the end of this report.

ship, in its more informal fellowship, in its organization and in the hospitality of the Christian home, there can be no place for exclusion or segregation because of race or color. "There is neither Jew nor Greek, bond nor free, for ye are all one in Christ." To allow the church's lines of action to be determined by racial discrimination denies the gospel whose proclamation is its task and commission.

(c) *The Church and the Common Life.* There is an urgent call to the church today to re-establish close relationships with the common life of the people in the midst of which it is called upon to work. The word of God must not only be preached; at any cost it must be made actual. Indeed only as it is thus being made actual can it be said to be completely preached. Today men are often more likely to criticize the church than to criticize Christianity; this is due in no small part to the fact that the church has lost touch with the everyday activities and problems which fill men's lives. To the outsider the church appears to be a society of people interested in a specialized activity which does not need and does not engage the interest of all. Religion is just one activity among many for those who are inclined that way. Men see no necessary relation between the moral struggles of society and the gospel of Christ. The church is not wholly to blame for this situation, since many spheres of the common life in which it once took the leading part have now been taken over by the community or by the state. But these changes only challenge the church to seek new areas and new means for the redemption of the common life.

3. SOME PRACTICAL SUGGESTIONS

There is a call from God today

(1) To every local congregation, to realize at any cost in its own self that unity, transcending all differences and

barriers of class, social status, race and nation, which we believe the Holy Spirit can and will create in those who are ready to be led by him.

(2) To different churches in any district, to come together for a local ecumenical witness in worship and work.

(3) To all Christians, to a more passionate and costly concern for the outcast, the underprivileged, the persecuted and the despised in the community and beyond the community. The recrudescence of pitiless cruelty, hatreds and race discriminations (including anti-Semitism) in the modern world is one of the major signs of its social disintegration. To these must be brought not the weak rebuke of words but the powerful rebuke of deeds. Thus the unity of the church is advanced. The church has been called into existence by God not for itself but for the world. Only by going out of itself in the work of Christ can it find unity in itself.

(4) More specifically to the church, to extend its concern to the particular areas of life where existing conditions continuously undo its work and thwart the will of God for his children — conditions such as misunderstanding between old and young, tension between men and women, health, housing, employment, recreation, in both their distinctive rural and urban forms. Thus the church seeks to express God's concern for every man in his own neighborhood and vocation.

(5) To the church, to undertake new social experiments, especially in local communities, through which the general level of conscience may be raised.

(6) To the church, to play a healing and reconciling part in the conflicts, misunderstandings or hatreds which arise between interests or classes within the local community or the nation.

(7) To the church, to encourage authoritative study of mooted problems in such areas as race and industry and to

draw together Christians of different races and groups for united study, fellowship and action.

(8) To Christian men and women in the same vocation or industry, to meet together for prayerful discussion as to how in their particular sphere of the common life the problems which arise can be dealt with as God would require.

(9) To members of the Christian church, to be ready to undertake responsibilities in local and national government. The church should seek to guide and support these its representatives in their efforts to solve the problems by which they are faced in the light of Christian principles.

(10) To all Christians, to seek by simplicity and discipline in personal living to go beyond the accepted standards of the community in the love revealed in Christ.

Finally, there is laid upon the Christian church in all lands the obligation to create and to foster among all its branches and among all its members solidarity and cooperation, which are stronger than all the divisions which now disrupt the family of mankind. The ecumenical movement which has found expression in the conference at Oxford should become an integral part in the life of every church, every local congregation and every individual Christian. To help to create it, to support it, to develop it, is a solemn responsibility to God who so loved the *world* that he gave his only begotten Son for its sin. Thus shall be plainly manifested to mankind in its chaos and division something of that peace and order of brotherly love which come only from God and from Jesus Christ his Son, our Lord.

SUPPLEMENTARY STATEMENT [3]

(1) "God wills all men to be saved." Therefore he has in Christ come to us, and therefore he has established

[3] See note on p. 16.

his church among us to proclaim the message of salvation through Christ for all nations. The church has the only all-decisive source for its message about God and his will in the revelation of God in Christ.

(2) As Christians we consider our membership in a distinct community (*Volk*) as a divine gift. The love of a Christian for his people is also his gratitude toward God for the gift thereby given to him.

(3) In order to fulfill its task the church takes its place in the community (*Volk*) wherein human life is lived. This does not mean the subordination of the church to the national life, but the effective fulfillment of its task to reach all members of the community with the gospel pure and undefiled.

(4) Every kind of national egotism, where the love of one's own nation leads to the suppression of other nationalities (minorities), is sin and rebellion against God, the Lord of all nations.

(5) The deification of one's own people is sin against God. "Thou shalt have none other God but me." To see in one's own people (in one's own blood) the saving revelation of God is anti-Christian. "Neither is there salvation in any other: for there is none other name under heaven given amongst men whereby we must be saved."

II. REPORT OF THE SECTION ON CHURCH AND STATE *

INTRODUCTION:
1. PURPOSE OF THE MEMORANDUM

IT IS NOT the purpose of the following memorandum to set forth an abstract doctrine of the relation of church and state either in sociological, legal or theological form, but to express the Christian's attitude toward the secularization of modern society and the growing power of the state, phenomena which present problems to the intelligence of Christians and lay burdens upon their consciences.

The purpose of this memorandum is to inquire what problems the existing situation presents to Christians both in their individual and in their corporate capacity, and to distinguish those principles and duties which determine the Christian attitude toward the state in all circumstances from the various applications of those principles and duties which are relevant to the different historical situations.

STANDPOINT:
2. FUNDAMENTAL CONSIDERATIONS

We speak as Christians, that is, (a) as members of the church as the body of Christ, the universal supra-national fellowship which he has called into being through his word

* The report, after receiving the approval of the section, was submitted to the conference substantially in its present form. The conference received the report, referred it back to the section for revision in the light of the discussion and commended it to the serious and favorable consideration of the churches. The report was revised by the section and approved by it in its present form.

and Spirit, or, in the words of the Apostles' Creed, the holy, catholic church; and (b) as members of the many particular churches — congregational, denominational, national, free or established — or other forms of Christian society in which the life of the one church finds varying expression.[1]

It follows (a) that our witness must be based upon the revelation which God has given us in Jesus Christ and in conformity with his word in the Scripture; and (b) that as human beings subject to the limitations of finiteness and the guilt of sin, we share responsibility for the evils of our time and must approach the subject of our relation to the state in a spirit of repentance.

We recognize that, both as members of individual churches and as members of the church universal, we are related to the particular states of which we are members, not only directly — as, e.g., by establishment or concordat — but primarily through the people of whom the state, whatever may be its constitutional structure, is the political organ. It follows that the special duties and responsibilities of the church with reference to the state are conditioned by all the aspects of the social life of man, economic, cultural, etc., with which church and state alike have to do.

We recognize the existing states as historically given realities, each of which in the political sphere is the highest authority, but which, as it stands itself under the authority and the judgment of God, is bound by his will and has the God-given aim of upholding law and order, of ministering to the life of the people united within it or of the peoples or groups so united, and also of making its contribution to the common life of all peoples.

[1] We recognize that, in addition to these uses, the word " church " is often loosely used to denote individual Christians or groups of Christians.

At the same time we recognize that the state as a specific form and the dominating expression of man's life in this world of sin, by its very power and its monopoly of the means of coercion often becomes an instrument of evil. Since we believe in the holy God as the source of justice, we do not consider the state as the ultimate source of law but rather as its guarantor. It is not the lord but the servant of justice. There can be for the Christian no ultimate authority but very God.

The state so defined has a dual relationship to the church, both as an order within which Christians have to live and witness for Christ; and as an institution which by its actions may either promote or hinder the mission of the church, in relation to which therefore the church in differing historical situations may be called to take differing positions of cooperation, criticism, or opposition, and this both in its corporate capacity and as a fellowship of witnessing Christians acting as individuals or as groups.

3. THE PRESENT SITUATION WITH REFERENCE TO CHURCH AND STATE

While the principles which define the Christian attitude toward the state remain always the same, their application has constantly varied in different countries and ages, not only because of changes in the organization and policy of different states but because of similar changes in different branches of the church. In any discussion of the relation of church and state, therefore, the historical situation must always be considered.

In the course of history church and state have taken very different attitudes toward each other, varying from the most intimate combination to complete indifference or antagonism. At the present time also their relations differ widely.

Furthermore, we have to distinguish among (*a*) states and countries with a predominantly Christian population; (*b*) states and countries with a population chiefly or at least largely de-Christianized; (*c*) states and countries with a non-Christian civilization where Christianity appears as the religion of a minority. We must distinguish also between churches which either completely or to a certain extent are organized independently of the state, and churches which are established.

There are two facts characteristic of the present situation which lay upon the church the duty of reconsidering its relation to the state and redefining its practical attitude. These are, first, the growing de-Christianization of society; second, the widespread tendency of the state to control the totality of human life in all its individual and social aspects, combined with the tendency to attribute absolute value to the state itself, to the national community, to the dominating class or to the prevailing cultural form.

4. THE CHURCH'S NEED OF REPENTANCE AND RECONSECRATION

The supreme duty of the churches in all countries as they face the present situation in the world of states and nations is to repent before God, not only by corporate acts of repentance, but by awakening the spirit of repentance in all their members: repentance for things done and things left undone. Judgment must begin at the house of God. If as Christians we are deeply disquieted by the political development of our age and our time, we have to acknowledge a large share of responsibility. We have not lived up to the word of our Lord: " Ye are the salt of the earth and the light of the world." We have not expressed our faith in the redeeming cross of Christ in terms of our social relations. We have accepted without clear protest existing social divisions. In like manner we recognize that churches have at times substituted for the true totalitarianism of Christ, which requires that every activity and every relation be subject to the will of God, a forced totalitarianism political in character. They have too often been far more concerned for their own security and prestige in this world than for fulfilling their Lord's commission and serving mankind in the spirit of self-sacrificing love. Today with deep humility we acknowledge our share in this guilt.

With repentance must go reconsecration. Penitence, if sincere, must bear fruit in action. We therefore resolve by God's grace to do our utmost to prevent the repetition of such sins in the future; to discharge our duties as citizens in the spirit of Christian love; and so far as in us lies, to create a spirit which will enable the state to fulfill its God-given task of maintaining justice and ministering to the welfare of the people.

PRINCIPLES:

5. THE DISTINCTIVE FUNCTIONS OF CHURCH AND OF STATE

The church as the trustee of God's redeeming gospel and the state as the guarantor of order, justice, and civil liberty have distinct functions in regard to society. The church's concern is to witness to men of the realities which outlast change because they are founded on the eternal will of God. The concern of the state is to provide men with justice, order and security in a world of sin and change. As it is the aim of the church to create a community founded on divine love, it cannot do its work by coercion, nor must it compromise the standards embodied in God's commandments by surrender to the necessities of the day. The state, on the other hand, has the duty of maintaining public order, and therefore must use coercion and accept the limits of the practicable.

The distinctive character of the church's activity is the free operation of grace and love. The distinctive character of the state's activity, whatever its constructive function in cultural and social life may be, is the power of constraint, legal and physical. In consequence there are certain social activities which clearly belong to the church and others which clearly belong to the state; there are, however, still others which may be performed by either church or state. In this area tension is unavoidable and solutions will vary in varying historical circumstances. It is true that our Lord told his disciples to render to Caesar the things that are Caesar's and to God the things that are God's. But it is God who declares what is Caesar's. Therefore, whatever the choice may be, the Christian must always, whether as a member of the church or as a citizen, obey the will of God.

6. DUTIES OF THE CHURCH TO THE STATE

The primary duty of the church to the state is to be the church, namely, to witness for God, to preach his word, to confess the faith before men, to teach both young and old to observe the divine commandments, and to serve the nation and the state by proclaiming the will of God as the supreme standard to which all human wills must be subject and all human conduct must conform. These functions of worship, preaching, teaching and ministry the church cannot renounce whether the state consent or not.

From this responsibility certain duties follow for the churches and for their members.

(a) *Duties with Reference to the Individual State.* These duties are (a) that of praying for the state, its people and its governments; (b) that of loyalty and obedience to the state, disobedience becoming a duty only if obedience would be clearly contrary to the command of God; (c) that of cooperation with the state in promoting the welfare of the citizens and of lending moral support to the state when it upholds the standards of justice set forth in the Word of God; (d) that of criticism of the state when it departs from those standards; (e) that of holding before men in all their legislation and administration those principles which make for the upholding of the dignity of man who is made in the image of God; (f) that of permeating the public life with the spirit of Christ and of training up men and women who as Christians can contribute to this end.

These duties rest upon Christians not only as individuals redeemed by Christ who must witness for him in whatever position they may occupy in the state, but also upon the church as a Christian community. The church can serve the state in no better way than by illustrating in its own life the kind of life which is God's will for society as a whole. Only in the measure that it seeks to realize this mission is it in a position to rebuke the state for its sins and failures for which both individual Christians and the church in its organized capacity have been in no small measure responsible.

(b) *Duties with Reference to the State in Its Relations to Other States.* In the interpretation of these duties it is important to keep constantly in mind that as the church in its own sphere is a universal society, so to Christian faith the individual state is not itself the ultimate political unit, but a member of a family of nations with international relations and duties which it is the responsibility not only of the individual Christians but also of the churches to affirm and to promote.

7. THE FREEDOM OF THE CHURCH

In a state which is Christian by profession it is self-evident that the church should be free to the fullest extent to fulfill its function. It should also be evident that where in such a state there are majority and minority churches the same essential liberty to carry out the church's function should be enjoyed by minorities as well as by the majority. All churches should renounce the use of the coercive power of the state in matters of religion. Membership in a minority church should not be a reason for denying full civil and political equality.

In a state which acknowledges a liberal doctrine of rights it is equally evident that the church like other associations should have the liberty which its function requires. In countries where the church finds in the theory and constitution of the state nothing on which to base a claim to right, this does not absolve the church from its primary duty of witness. This duty must then include a witness against such a denial of fundamental justice. And if the state tries to hinder or suppress such witness, all other churches have the duty of supporting this church and giving it the utmost succor and relief in their power.

We recognize as essential conditions necessary to the church's fulfillment of its primary duty that it should enjoy: (a) freedom to determine its faith and creed; (b) freedom of public and private worship, preaching and teaching; (c) freedom from any imposition by the state of religious ceremonies and forms of worship; (d) freedom to determine the nature of its government and the qualifications of its ministers and members and, conversely, the freedom of the individual to join the church to which he feels called; (e) freedom to control the education of its ministers, to give religious instruction to its youth and to provide for adequate development of their religious life; (f) freedom of Christian service and missionary activity, both home and foreign; (g) freedom to cooperate with other churches; (h) freedom to use such facilities, open to all citizens or associations, as will make possible the accomplishment of these ends: the ownership of property and the collection of funds.

The freedom essential for the church can in fact exist both in churches organized as free associations under the general laws of a country and in churches established in an organic or other special connection with the state. If, however, this connection should result in impairing the church's freedom to carry out its distinctive mission, it would then become the duty of its ministers and members to do all in their power to secure this freedom, even at the cost of disestablishment.

8. THE PRESENT TASKS OF THE CHURCH

What then follows from this survey as to the present tasks and opportunities of the churches? This at least, that it is their duty:

(1) To summon their own members to repentance, both as individuals and as organized bodies, for their sins of omission and of commission and to pray for the spirit of consecration which shall make of them, both in their separate and in their united activities, agents which God may use for his purpose in the world.

(2) To create within the local community, the nation, and the world such agencies of cooperative action as shall make it possible for them to discharge effectively such tasks as can be done in common.

(3) To summon their individual members in their several callings — not only clerical but also lay members, men and women — to cooperate with the state in such constructive tasks as may be for the good of the whole.

(4) To guard for all churches, both as groups of witnessing Christians and in their organized capacity, the oppor-

tunity of worship, of witness, of service, and of education which is essential to their mission, and this not for their own sake only, but for the sake of the states.

(5) To follow with sympathetic interest the fortunes of those, Christians and non-Christians, who are victims of cruelty and oppression, and to do what they can to secure for them a treatment compatible with the dignity of their human personality as children of God.

(6) To renounce publicly and forever the use of all forms of persecution, whether by Christians against other Christians or by Christians against adherents of other religions.

III. REPORT OF THE SECTION ON CHURCH, COMMUNITY AND STATE IN RELATION TO THE ECONOMIC ORDER *

1. THE BASIS OF THE CHRISTIAN CONCERN FOR THE ECONOMIC ORDER

THE CHRISTIAN church approaches the problems of the social and economic order from the standpoint of her faith in the revelation of God in Christ. In the life and death of our Lord, God is revealed as a just God who condemns sin and as a merciful God who redeems sinners. The nature and will of God as thus revealed form the basis of human existence and the standard of human conduct. The chief end of man is to glorify God, to honor and love him, in work and life as in worship. This love involves the obligation to love our neighbors as ourselves, a second commandment which Jesus declared to be like unto the first.

This love of neighbor is an obligation which rests partly upon the native worth and dignity of man as made in the image of God. In all systems of morality this obligation is to a greater or less degree recognized. Christianity, however, recognizes that the image of God in man is so defaced by sin that man's native worth and dignity are largely obscured. For this reason it must be emphasized that our obligation to the neighbor springs not so much from our recognition of man's native dignity as from the Christian

* This report was the first to be presented to the full conference and was submitted in shorter form. The conference received the report, referred it back to the section for revision in the light of the discussion and commended it to the serious and favorable consideration of the churches. The report was revised and expanded by the section and approved in its present form by all the members present at the final meeting of the section.

revelation of God's purpose to restore that dignity through the redemption that is in Christ. The obligation is therefore a duty toward God and continues to be operative even when the neighbor does not obviously demand or deserve respect. We must love our fellow men because God loves them and wills to redeem them.

The kingdom of God, as proclaimed in the gospel, is the reign of God which both has come and is coming. It is an established reality in the coming of Christ and in the presence of his Spirit in the world. It is, however, still in conflict with a sinful world which crucified its Lord, and its ultimate triumph is still to come. In so far as it has come, the will of God as revealed in Christ (that is, the commandment of love) is the ultimate standard of Christian conduct. Standards drawn from the observation of human behavior or prompted by immediate necessities are not only less complete than the commandment of love but frequently contain elements that contradict it. In so far as the kingdom of God is in conflict with the world and is therefore still to come, the Christian finds himself under the necessity of discovering the best available means of checking human sinfulness and of increasing the possibilities and opportunities of love within a sinful world.

The relative and departmental standard for all the social arrangements and institutions, all the economic structures and political systems, by which the life of man is ordered is the principle of justice. Justice, as the ideal of a harmonious relation of life to life, obviously presupposes the sinful tendency of one life to take advantage of another. This sinful tendency it seeks to check by defining the rightful place and privilege which each life must have in the harmony of the whole and by assigning the duty of each to each. Justice does not demand that the self *sacrifice* itself completely for the neighbor's good, but seeks to define and to maintain the good which each member of the community may rightfully claim in the harmony of the whole.

The principle of justice has both a positive and a negative significance. Negatively, principles of justice restrain evil and the evildoer. They must therefore become embodied in systems of coercion which prevent men from doing what sinful ambition, pride, lust and greed might prompt them to do. This necessary coercion is itself a root of new evils, since its exercise involves power and power tempts the possessor to its unrighteous use. Furthermore, coercion may rouse resentment among those coerced even when its purpose is a necessary social end. The use of power and coercion cannot therefore be regarded by Christians as ultimately desirable. Criticism against its abuses must be constantly maintained. On the other hand, it cannot be assumed that the practice of Christian love will ever obviate the necessity for coercive political and economic arrangements.

The laws of justice are not purely negative. They are not merely " dikes against sin." The political and economic structure of society is also the mechanical skeleton which carries the organic element in society. Forms of production and methods of cooperation may serve the cause of human brotherhood by serving and extending the principle of love beyond the sphere of purely personal relations.

The commandment of love therefore always presents possibilities for individuals beyond the requirements of economic and social institutions. There is no legal, political or economic system so bad or so good as to absolve individuals from the responsibility to transcend its requirements by acts of Christian charity. Institutional requirements necessarily prescribe only the minimum. Even in the best possible social system they can only achieve general standards in which the selfishness of the human heart is taken for granted and presupposed. But the man who is in Christ knows a higher obligation which transcends the requirements of justice — the obligation of a love which is the fulfillment of the law.

The love which is the fulfillment of the law is, however, no substitute for law, for institutions or for systems. Individual acts of charity within a given system of government or economics may mitigate its injustices and increase its justice. But they do not absolve the Christian from seeking the best possible institutional arrangement and social structure for the ordering of human life. Undue emphasis upon the higher possibilities of love in personal relations, within the limits of a given system of justice or an established social structure, may tempt Christians to allow individual acts of charity to become a screen for injustice and a substitute for justice. Christianity becomes socially futile if it does not recognize that love must will justice and that the Christian is under an obligation to secure the best possible social and economic structure, in so far as such structure is determined by human decisions.

The relation of the commandment of love to the justice of political and economic systems is twofold. It is an ideal which reaches beyond any possible achievements in the field of political relations, but it is nevertheless also a standard by which various schemes of justice may be judged. In attempting to deal with political and economic problems, the Christian must therefore be specially on his guard against two errors.

The one is to regard the realities of social justice incorporated in given systems and orders as so inferior to the law of love that the latter cannot be a principle of discrimination among them but only a principle of indiscriminate judgment upon them all. This error makes Christianity futile as a guide in all those decisions which Christians, like other people, must constantly be making in the political and economic sphere. Practically, it gives the advantage to established systems as against the challenge of new social adventures and experiments; for it tempts Christians to make no decisions at all, and such efforts to reserve decision become in practice decisions in favor of the status quo.

The other error is to identify some particular social system with the will of God or to equate it with the kingdom of God. When conservatives insist on such an identification in favor of the status quo, they impart to it a dangerous religious sanction which must drive those who challenge it into a secular revolt against religion itself. If, on the other hand, this identification is made in the interests of a new social order, it will lead to the same complacency which the critic deprecates in the old social situation. Every tendency to identify the kingdom of God with a particular social structure or economic mechanism must result in moral confusion for those who maintain the system and in disillusionment for those who suffer from its limitations. The former will regard conformity with its standards as identical with the fulfillment of the law, thus falling into the sin of pharisaism. The latter will be tempted to a cynical disavowal of the religion because it falsely gives absolute worth to partial values and achievements. Both errors are essentially heretical from the point of view of Christian faith. The one denies the reality of the kingdom of God in history; the other equates the kingdom of God with the processes of history. In the one case, the ultimate and eternal destiny of human existence, which transcends history, is made to support an attitude of indifference toward historical social issues; in the other case, the eternal destiny of human existence is denied or obscured. The law of love which is the standard of the Christian life is properly to be regarded as being at the same time a present reality and an ultimate possibility. It is not only a criterion of judgment in all the fateful decisions which men must make in history, but also an indictment against all historical achievements.

As a criterion of judgment upon the relative merits of economic arrangements and social structures, the law of love gives positive guidance in terms of justice, even though it transcends the realities of all possible social structures. The obligation to love our neighbors as ourselves places clearly under condemnation all social and economic systems which give one man undue advantage over others. It must create an uneasy conscience (for example) in all Christians who are involved in a social system which denies children, of whatever race or class, the fullest opportunity to develop whatever gifts God has given them and makes their education depend upon the fortuitous circumstance of a father's possession or lack of means to provide the necessary funds. It must challenge any social system which provides social privileges without reference to the social functions performed by individuals, or which creates luxury and pride on the one hand and want and insecurity on the other. It makes the conscience of Christians particularly uneasy in regard to the deprivation of basic security for large masses of human beings.

2. ANALYSIS OF THE PRESENT ECONOMIC SITUATION

There is today no *one* economic order which ecumenical Christianity faces. The government of the U.S.S.R., for example, exercises jurisdiction over one-sixth of all the land surface of the globe, on which lives one-twelfth of the world's population, including — it has been estimated — one-fifth of the population of the industrialized world. The economic and social structure of this huge territory is fundamentally different from that prevailing elsewhere.

Again, national socialist Germany and fascist Italy have evolved economic systems each of which differs in important respects from those of other so-called capitalist countries. And between the types of capitalism which are evolving in democratic states — the Scandinavian countries, France, the United States, Great Britain, etc. — there are also differences of a highly important kind. The amount, for instance, of social and industrial legislation which has been passed in Great Britain, and the extent to which trade unions have for many years been recognized there, make the economic system of that country very different from that found in the United States. For the present purpose it seems wise to concentrate attention on what can broadly be described as the capitalist economic system, though it must always be borne in mind not only that this phrase is liable to be dangerously misleading but also that a large part of the world lies outside its ambit.

The present economic situation in the countries under consideration is a product of the emancipation of the individual from the social and cultural restrictions of the Middle Ages. In so far as the spirit and the institutions of the feudal order and of the guild system had restrained, in spite of their religious and cultural creativity, the free development of human potentialities, the dawning of the capitalist age must be considered a definite step forward in the progress of humanity. This is true of the intellectual as well as of the political and economic achievements of that age. The system of free enterprise is responsible for that industrial development which, for the first time in human history, has made it possible to overcome the natural scarcity of economic resources by successive technological improvements. Despite the vast increase of the world's population, it has raised to a considerable degree the general standard of consumption. By the mechanization of industry it has reduced the physical labor of the manual workers. For the first time in history it has brought all parts of the world into interdependence with one another and has made the idea of the unity of mankind a fact of common experience.

It was thought at one time that the development of this new economic order would not only improve the material conditions of life but would also establish social justice. This expectation was rooted in the belief that a pre-established harmony would so govern the self-interest of individuals as to create the greatest possible harmony in society as a whole. " Each man, seeking his own, would serve the commonweal." Today this belief is largely discredited. The attempt of human reason to create an autonomous and universal culture has resulted in a variety of independent and specialized cultural activities which are not related to any one organizing principle and which consequently lack that unity which we believe can be realized only through the penetration of the whole by the spirit of religion. The absence of this spiritual center from the economic order has involved the progressive dissipation of the spiritual inheritance of Western life. The same forces which have produced material progress have often enhanced inequalities, created permanent insecurity and subjected all members of modern society to the domination of so-called independent economic " laws." The competitive superiority of large-scale production has gone far to destroy the old traditional society of craftsmen and farmers and thereby has created a society which is characterized in many countries by the concentration of wealth on the one hand and the existence of large urban masses on the other. The progressive mechanization of industry has periodically thrown large numbers of workers into long periods of unemployment. The cycle of industrial fluctuations has caused a tremendous waste of productive power and, in consequence, " poverty in the midst of plenty."

At the same time the human side of economic life has been profoundly affected. Broadly speaking, capitalistic production has not escaped the danger of treating human labor as a commodity to be bought at the lowest possible price and to be utilized to the greatest possible extent. The predominance of the profit motive has tended to deprive the worker of the social meaning of his work and has encouraged hostility between the members of different groups in their economic relationships.

In the course of the nineteenth century the worst evils which accompanied the rise of capitalism were mitigated in the more advanced industrial nations. There was a rapid growth in the population of the industrialized part of the world, and the constant expansion of markets in industrially undeveloped countries reduced the social and economic pressure in the industrialized countries. These trade outlets made it possible to satisfy many of the demands of the poorer sections of the community by the increase of real wages and by social legislation in various fields. Under social and political pressure the various governments of the Western world enacted laws providing for graduated taxation and for old-age pensions, sickness and accident insurance, etc. The success of the trade unions and the cooperative movement helped also in this process of mitigation of social evils.

But industrial expansion and technical progress have tended to defeat their own ends. In place of free trade and free competition, which were characteristic principles of the earlier expansionist period of capitalism, protectionist measures were adopted by the state and monopolies were established in many fields of economic enterprise. One of the causes of this change lay in the fact that formerly

" backward " and colonial nations had become industrial competitors. The consequent contraction of markets accentuated the competition of nations for the remaining markets of the world. Through this development, the earlier stage of competitive capitalism has been gradually replaced by a monopolistic stage, and this economic change has brought with it corresponding political consequences. On the one hand, the economic process has been increasingly subjected to state control and interference; and on the other hand leading industrial and financial groups have been tempted to obtain the support of the state for their particular interests, and the original ideal of modern democracy has thus in practice become increasingly difficult to achieve.

The World War and its economic consequences have accelerated and accentuated these tendencies, not only within the economy of particular nations but also in the relationship of state to state. As the former outlets for economic expansion have become progressively more narrow, the fundamental tensions of the capitalistic economic order are becoming increasingly manifest to our generation. The older tendency toward free competition remains a factor in all Western nations and contends against the new tendency toward monopoly and state control. Out of this conflict social and economic systems have emerged in the different nations which contain elements of both tendencies in varying proportions.

While the agrarian population participated in the benefits of capitalistic expansion in the latter nineteenth century, the recent mechanization of agricultural production has also drawn predominantly agrarian areas in many parts of the world into a rapid process of transformation.

This brief survey would be incomplete without calling attention to the effect of capitalistic development upon countries, such as China and India, which had not been active participants in the process. Their observation of the process in other nations and their reaction to economic exploitation by capitalistic powers have prompted a widespread demand for radical social change through which the benefits of industrialization might be secured and the evils from which the industrialized nations of the West are suffering might be avoided.

A consequence of this development of capitalism was the rise of socialism and communism. These movements represent a protest against the evil results of the capitalist economic order from those who suffered chiefly from it. In several countries this protest allied itself with a radical denial of Christianity, the church and belief in God. This denial is *partly* due to the fact that the churches had become deeply involved in the social and cultural attitudes of the wealthier members of society, upon whom they were frequently dependent politically and economically. As the churches did not detach themselves from these alliances a disastrous chasm opened between those who were struggling for social justice but on nonreligious or antireligious grounds, and those who stood for the Christian faith but did not seem to recognize existing injustices. This is one of the reasons why victorious communism persecutes the Christian churches, denounces religion as a tool of reaction and seeks to eradicate it; and why in other countries the ruthless persecution of communists and socialists is either tolerated without protest or supported by Christians and churches.

Facing this situation the Christian churches must first of all acknowledge and repent for their blindness to the actual situation; for this blindness is partly responsible for such hostility as exists between themselves and the radical movements which aim at social justice. The churches must not regard an attack directed against themselves as an attack directed against God. They must acknowledge that God has spoken to their conscience through these movements by revealing through them the real situation of millions of their members. On the other hand, the churches must continue resolutely to reject those elements in the actual development of communism which conflict with the Christian truth: the *utopianism* which looks for the fulfillment of human existence through the natural process of history and presupposes that improvement of social institutions will automatically produce improvement in human personalities; the *materialism* which derives all moral and spiritual values from economic needs and economic conditions and deprives the personal and cultural life of its creative freedom; and, finally, the *disregard for the dignity of the individual* in which communism may differ theoretically, but does not differ practically, from other contemporary totalitarian movements.

3. POINTS AT WHICH THE CHRISTIAN UNDERSTANDING OF LIFE IS CHALLENGED

At the beginning of this part of the report attention should be called to the potentialities for good in the economic order. Situations vary in different parts of the world but in many countries it already seems possible, through the full utilization of the resources of the new technology and through the release of human productive power, to remove the kind of poverty which is crippling to human personality. There is a sense in which poverty is a relative matter and hence in any situation would be present in some form; but we are thinking of the poverty which would be regarded in any age as denying the physical necessities of life. The abolition of such poverty now seems to depend on the human organization of economic life, rather than on factors given in nature or on what might be called the inevitable constitution of every economic order. But the possibility of economic "plenty" has this moral importance, that to an increasing extent it makes the persistence of poverty a matter for which men are morally responsible. This possibility marks off our time from the period of the New Testament and from other periods in which Christian thinking about economic life has been formulated. In the light of it the direction of Christian effort in relation to the economic order should henceforth be turned from charitable paternalism to the realization of more equal justice in the distribution of wealth. Moreover, Christians who live in the more privileged geographical areas must recognize that the securing of economic plenty and greater justice in its distribution within their respective national groups is not the whole of their duty in this connection; they cannot escape some measure of responsibility for those areas where for years to come there will doubtless be desperate economic need.

It seems to us that the moral and spiritual nature of man, according to the Christian understanding of that nature, is affronted by the assumptions and operation of the economic order of the industrialized world in four respects to which we wish to draw special attention.

(a) *The Enhancement of Acquisitiveness.* That economic order results, in the first place, in a serious danger that the finer qualities of the human spirit will be sacrificed to an overmastering preoccupation with a department of life which, though important on its own plane, ought to be strictly subordinated to other more serious aspects of life. We are warned by the New Testament that riches are a danger to their possessors, and experience would appear to confirm that diagnosis. It is not possible to serve both God and Mammon. When the necessary work of society is so organized as to make the acquisition of wealth the chief criterion of success, it encourages a feverish scramble for money, and a false respect for the victors in the struggle which is as fatal in its moral consequences as any other form of idolatry. In so far as the pursuit of monetary gain becomes the dominant factor in the lives of men, the quality of society undergoes a subtle disintegration. That such a society should be the scene of a perpetual conflict of interests, sometimes concealed, sometimes overt, between the economic groups composing them, is not surprising. Men can cooperate only in so far as they are united by allegiance to a common purpose which is recognized as superior to their sectional interests. As long as industry is organized primarily not for the service of the community but with the object of producing a purely financial result for some of its members, it cannot be recognized as properly fulfilling its social purpose.

(b) *Inequalities.* The second feature of the economic system which challenges the conscience of Christians is the existence of disparities of economic circumstance on a scale which differs from country to country, but in some is shocking, in all considerable. Not only is the product of industry distributed with an inequality so extreme (though the extent of this inequality also varies considerably from country to country) that a small minority of the population are in receipt of incomes exceeding in the aggregate those of many times their number, but — even more seriously — the latter are condemned throughout their lives to environmental evils which the former escape, and are deprived of the opportunities of fully developing their powers which are accessible, as a matter of course, to their more fortunate fellows. It is no part of the teaching of Christianity that all men are equally endowed by nature or that identical provision should be made for all, irrespective of difference

of capacity and need. What Christianity does assert is that
all men are children of one Father, and that, compared with
that primary and overwhelming fact, the differences between the races, nationalities and classes of men, though
important on their own plane, are external and trivial.
Any social arrangement which outrages the dignity of man
by treating some men as ends and others as means, any institution which obscures the common humanity of men by
emphasizing the external accidents of birth or wealth or
social position, is *ipso facto* anti-Christian.

One aspect of the matter deserves special emphasis.
Whatever their differences on other subjects, Christians
cannot be in doubt as to the primary duty of insuring that
the conditions required for full personal development are
enjoyed by the whole of the rising generation. In some
countries that obligation receives fuller recognition than
in others, but of few, if any, can it be said that equal opportunities of physical and mental growth are available for
all. It is still the case, even in some of the wealthy nations
of western Europe, that large numbers of children undergo
grave injury to their health before they reach the age of
school attendance, though the methods by which such injury can be prevented are well known; that the education
given them at school is often, owing to reluctance to spend
the sums required, gravely defective in quality; that many
of them are plunged prematurely into full-time work in
industry, where too often they are employed under conditions injurious both to their characters and to their physical well-being; and that diversities of educational provision
correspond to differences of income among parents rather
than of capacity among children. It often happens that
these disadvantages are greatly increased where economic
opportunities are denied on racial grounds. This racial
discrimination is seen in various forms: a double standard

of wages; the inability of members of certain races, whatever their competence may be, to rise above a certain level of responsibility in their respective callings; their exclusion in some circumstances from labor unions; and the refusal to admit members of some racial groups to occupations reserved for members of the dominant race.

(c) *Irresponsible Possession of Economic Power.* A third feature of the existing situation which is repugnant to the Christian conscience consists in the power wielded by a few individuals or groups who are not responsible to any organ of society. This gives the economic order in many countries some resemblance to a tyranny, in the classical sense of that term, where rulers are not accountable for their actions to any superior authority representing the community over whom power is exercised. At the top of this hierarchy are the leaders of the world of finance, whose decisions raise and lower the economic temperature. Below them are the controllers of certain great key industries, the conduct and policy of which vitally affect the lives of millions of human beings. Below them again are a mass of economic undertakings, large and small, the masters of which exercise power over the few hundred or few thousand persons dependent on each of them. The power which these latter wield is qualified at many points by trade unionism and by the law. On the whole, however, the action both of trade unionism and of the state has been confined hitherto to establishing and maintaining certain minimum standards. Almost the whole field of economic strategy, which in the long run determines what standards can be maintained, escapes their control.

Economic like political autocracy is attended doubtless by certain advantages. However, it is liable to produce both in individuals and in society a character and an outlook on life which it is difficult to reconcile with any relationship that can be described as Christian. It tends to create in those who wield authority, and in the agents through whom they exercise it, a dictatorial temper which springs not from any defect of character peculiar to them but from the influence upon them of the position they occupy. The effect of excessive economic power on those over whom it is exercised is equally serious. Often it makes them servile; fear of losing their jobs, and a vague belief that in the end the richer members of society always hold the whip hand, tends to destroy their spiritual virility. Often, again, it makes them bitter and cynical; they feel that force, not justice, rules their world, and they are tempted to dismiss as insincere cant words which imply a different view.

(d) *The Frustration of the Sense of Christian Vocation.* A profound conflict has arisen between the demand that the Christian should be doing the will of God in his daily work, and the actual kinds of work which Christians find themselves forced to do within the economic order. With regard to the worker and employee, there is the fact that most of them are *directly* conscious of working for the profit of the employer (and for the sake of their wages) and only *indirectly* conscious of working for any public good; while this fact may in some cases be only part of the mechanism by which the work is done for the public good, the difficulty in some degree remains. Again, there is the fact that at present many workers must produce things which are useless or shoddy or destructive. Finally, one other form of work which seems clearly to be in conflict with the Christian's vocation is salesmanship of a kind which involves deception — the deception which may be no more than insinuation and exaggeration, but which is a serious threat to the integrity of the worker.

But even more serious is the constant threat of unemployment. This produces a feeling of extreme insecurity in the minds of masses of the people. Unemployment, especially when prolonged, tends to create in the mind of the unemployed person a sense of uselessness or even of being a nuisance, and to empty his life of any meaning. This situation cannot be met by measures of unemployment assistance, because it is the lack of significant activity which tends to destroy his human self-respect.

4. CHRISTIAN DECISIONS IN RESPONSE TO THIS CHALLENGE

It was pointed out in the first section of this report that the message of the gospel is not addressed, as has sometimes been suggested, to the individual alone. Christianity is emphatically a social religion. Its teaching is directed to men not as units isolated from their fellows but as members of groups and communities. It insists that the only life in which human beings can find peace and happiness is that of service and self-sacrifice. It asserts that the relations of men to one another are part of their relation to God. It emphasizes that, if the former are not what the Christian conscience would approve, then the latter necessarily share their corruption. " If a man love not his brother whom he hath seen, how shall he love God whom he hath not seen? "

These relations are, of course, of many different kinds. But in the case of the majority of men they are determined more directly and more continuously by the action of economic interests than by any other single force. It is clearly the duty of Christians, therefore, to test by the canons of their faith not merely their individual conduct and the quality of their private lives, but also the institutional framework of organized society. In so far as they are true to their creed, they cannot either take the economic system for granted or dismiss it as irrelevant to the life of the spirit. They are bound to require it to present its moral credentials; to examine those credentials in the light of

Christian doctrine as to the nature of God and man; and, in so far as the system fails to satisfy that criterion, to use every effort to amend or to supersede it. If detachment is incumbent on Christians in reaching their conclusions, courage in stating and energy in acting on them are no less among their duties.

Whatever agreements may be reached by Christians concerning their responsibility for seeking to eradicate those features of the economic order which challenge the Christian conscience, it is an historic fact, which we can hardly expect to obviate in the future, that men who belong to the Christian church and who are united by common religious convictions differ in the conception and in the execution of their political obligations. The profoundest difference at the present time in many countries seems to be between those who believe that the challenges to the Christian faith outlined in the previous section can be met within the framework of a system of private enterprise, and those who demand the supplanting of that system by one primarily based upon the social ownership of the means of production. But even within these two general divisions of opinion, other differences of great importance about the precise means of improving the present system, or about the tempo and the degree of reconstruction needed, have revealed themselves in the work of this conference. These differences are an accurate reflection, we believe, of similar differences in the whole church.

These differences are of course partly differences of judgment such as honest minds face in any realm of human decision. But it must be recognized also that differences in political opinion are partly derived from the varying circumstances — economic, geographic and historical — which help to condition human judgments. Human judgments upon issues in which our own lives are involved are naturally less impartial than those which concern purely objective problems. The very recognition of this fact within the church might well mitigate the extremism to which each group is tempted. If those who are comparatively secure recognize the temptation to complacency which this security implies, the temper of the insecure may speak to their conscience and not merely excite their temper. On the other hand, the proponents of a new social system are always tempted to identify every existing evil with the particular social organization in which it expresses itself. They find it difficult to disassociate perennial human sinfulness from particular historic forms of it. They are furthermore tempted to a hatred toward the representatives of a given social order which is not justified by the facts, since evils in it are only partly willed and partly the inevitable consequence of a given social situation which good men may mitigate but not overcome. Thus there are at least two attitudes toward political and economic problems which seem to be definitely incompatible with membership in the Christian church: the complacent defense of exclusive privilege on the one hand, and unteachable and self-righteous fanaticism on the other.

Among the various proposals for reform or reconstruction of the economic system several deserve special mention here. Within terms of the present system, the various proposals may be generally reduced to two: (*a*) Those which look toward exerting a greater degree of social and political control upon, and demanding a greater degree of social responsibility from, the holders of great economic power. (*b*) Those which seek to equalize the inequalities of economic society by heavy taxation on the one hand and by social legislation on the other. Every modern industrial nation has adopted these two social policies to a greater or less degree. A third policy, that of seeking to prevent

e centralization of power by government destruction of
onopoly and by government support of small farmers,
small traders, etc., is less popular in all industrial nations
an it was some decades ago. All these policies point to a
cognition that the chief dangers of a system of private
nterprise are irresponsible power and inequality.

Among those who believe in the transformation or re-
nstruction of a system of private enterprise to one of
cial ownership, there are wide varieties of conviction on
e means and tempo of this process of reconstruction.
here is a general hope that this can be done by gradual
rocess and through the resources of democratic political
rms. Nevertheless some feel that, however desirable it
ay be to make all social decisions through the democratic
rocess, there is no way of guaranteeing the acquiescence of
inorities, upon which the democratic process depends.
hey point out that in moments of great social crisis every
ciety must deal with the possibility that minorities,
hether conservative or radical, may defy rather than submit to the will of the majority. But recent Russian history offers such telling examples of the danger of irresponsible political power, supplanting irresponsible economic
power when the democratic control of power is destroyed,
that the determination of the nations which still possess
democratic forms to preserve and maintain them has been
greatly reinforced.

There remains among proponents of social ownership a
wide variety of opinion on the degree of socialization of
property required by a technical civilization. Most generally it is the basic industries and the natural resources for
which such socialization is demanded. The socialization
of land, of retail trade and of small industry finds fewer
proponents, though the first is an issue wherever feudal
forms of landownership and tenantry are still in existence.

There are certain social proposals which fall between the policy of maintaining the system of private property and that of socializing it. Chief among these are the proposals for the socialization of money and credit and for the extension of the principle of cooperation through voluntary cooperative enterprises. Both of these have secured particularly strong support among Christian people on the ground that they offer the opportunity of eliminating the evils of the present system in a more thoroughgoing fashion while they involve less social conflict and tension. The question which the first proposal must answer is whether money and credit are more organically related to property than it assumes. The second proposal must answer the question whether cooperatives, which have thus far developed only in the realm of consumers' goods, can affect in any way the problems of heavy industry.

All of these proposals involve technical issues upon which technical evidence varies, and it is therefore impossible to claim a moral obligation in support of any of them. There is always the possibility that new institutions will reintroduce ancient evils in a new form or substitute new evils for those which have been abolished. Such a question involves technical problems on which Christians as Christians are not competent to pronounce. It would be well however for Christians to beware lest the weight which is accorded to technical evidence in the support or rejection of any one proposal be determined by the particular bias of the social group to which they belong.

The Christian church is a fellowship in Christ which transcends differences of judgment and divergences of action in relation to the concrete economic situation. Further, if only Christians are brought to repentance in the light of the Christian message, they can never maintain that attitude of fanatical hatred toward members of other groups which is now so common in the world. They and their opponents are both sinners in the presence of God, and the recognition of this fact, in social as well as in personal terms, would itself be a great constructive contribution toward moderating the bitterness of the struggle between social groups.

5. CHRISTIAN TEACHING IN RELATION TO THE ECONOMIC ORDER

We stated in the third section of this report the special points at which there is a conflict between the present economic order and the Christian understanding of life. In the next section we pointed out the kind of social decisions which have to be made by all Christians as citizens.

But it is not enough to say that these problems are chiefly the responsibility of Christian individuals or Christian lay groups and leave the matter there. The further question must be raised: What guidance can those who must make these decisions concerning the economic order receive from their Christian faith? That question places great responsibility upon those in the church who have the task of interpreting the meaning of Christian faith. In this work of interpretation the clergy should have a specially important contribution to make, but that contribution must be made with understanding of the experience of laymen. It is important that whenever this Christian guidance is crystallized in the reports and pronouncements of official church bodies, or of such a conference as the Oxford Conference, laymen should share with the clergy this task of formulation. These laymen should come from various economic groups. This section of the report will be an attempt to formulate the kind of guidance which it is now possible to receive from Christian faith for economic life. We are here dealing directly with what the teaching of the church as a church should be concerning the economic order.

We must begin by recognizing that there are some factors in economic life which are more clearly within the province of the church and concerning which more light can be gained from the Christian message than others, and that there are many matters of judgment in particular situations which involve chiefly expert knowledge. Recognizing, then, the importance of attempting to mark out as clearly as possible the precise areas within which the Christian can expect to receive light from the Christian faith and within which the teaching of the church as church in regard to economic life should be carried on, we proceed to suggest three such areas. In presenting these areas we are suggesting what might be the framework of the Christian message in relation to the economic order in the next decade.

(1) *Christian teaching should deal with ends, in the sense of long-range goals, standards and principles in the light of which every concrete situation and every proposal for improving it must be tested.* It is in the light of such ends and principles that the four characteristics of the existing economic order discussed in section two stand out as challenges to the Christian church. There are differences in theory concerning the way in which these ends are related to the Christian faith. Some would be very careful not to call these ends Christian and yet they would recognize that they are ends which *Christians* should seek in obedience to God.

We suggest five such ends or standards, by way of example, as applicable to the testing of any economic situation.

(a) Right fellowship between man and man being a

condition of man's fellowship with God, every economic arrangement which frustrates or restricts it must be modified — and in particular such ordering of economic life as tends to divide the community into classes based upon differences of wealth and to occasion a sense of injustice among the poorer members of society. To every member of the community there must be made open a worthy means of livelihood. The possibilities of amassing private accumulations of wealth should be so limited that the scale of social values is not perverted by the fear and the envy, the insolence and the servility, which tend to accompany extreme inequality.

(b) Regardless of race or class every child and youth must have opportunities of education suitable for the full development of his particular capacities, and must be free from those adventitious handicaps in the matter of health and environment which our society loads upon large numbers of the children of the less privileged classes. In this connection, the protection of the family as a social unit should be an urgent concern of the community.

(c) Persons disabled from economic activity, whether by sickness, infirmity or age, should not be economically penalized on account of their disability, but on the contrary should be the object of particular care. Here again the safeguarding of the family is involved.

(d) Labor has intrinsic worth and dignity, since it is designed by God for man's welfare. The duty and the right of men to work should therefore alike be emphasized. In the industrial process, labor should never be considered a mere commodity. In their daily work men should be able to recognize and fulfill a Christian vocation. The workingman, whether in field or factory, is entitled to a living wage, wholesome surroundings and a recognized voice in the decisions which affect his welfare as a worker.

(e) The resources of the earth, such as the soil and mineral wealth, should be recognized as gifts of God to the whole human race and used with due and balanced consideration for the needs of the present and future generations.

The implications of even one of these standards, seriously taken, will involve drastic changes in economic life. Each one of them must be made more definite in terms of the problems which face particular communities.

Closely connected with the foregoing paragraphs is the whole question of property — so closely indeed that any action on the part of the community which affects property rights will also affect the application of the standards mentioned. This is a sphere in which Christian teaching on ends and principles in relation to economic life could have immediate results if it were translated into actual economic decisions. Christian thought has already supplied a background which is of great importance, but it has not been brought into effective relationship with the development of the institutions of property under modern economic conditions. This subject should be given close attention by any agencies for further study which may be established in the future. Meanwhile we suggest a few of the directions along which Christian thought should move.

(a) It should be reaffirmed without qualification that all human property rights are relative and contingent only, in virtue of the dependence of man upon God as the giver of all wealth and as the creator of man's capacities to develop the resources of nature. This fundamental Christian conviction must express itself both in the idea of stewardship or trusteeship and in the willingness of the Christian to examine accumulations of property in the light of their social consequences.

(b) The existing system of property rights and the existing distribution of property must be criticized in the light of the largely nonmoral processes by which they have been developed, and criticism must take account of the fact that every argument in defense of property rights which is valid for Christian thinking is also an argument for the widest possible distribution of these rights.

(c) It should further be affirmed that individual property rights must never be maintained or exercised without regard to their social consequences or without regard to the contribution which the community makes in the production of all wealth.

(d) It is very important to make clear distinction between various forms of property. The property which consists in personal possessions for use, such as the home, has behind it a clearer moral justification than property in the means of production and in land which gives the owners power over other persons. All property which represents social power stands in special need of moral scrutiny, since power to determine the lives of others is the crucial point in any scheme of justice. The question must always be asked whether this is the kind of power which can be brought under adequate social control or whether it is of the type which by its very nature escapes and evades social control. Industrial property in particular encourages the concentration of power; for it gives the owner control over both the place and the instruments of labor and thus leaves the worker powerless so far as property relations are concerned, allowing him only the organized strength of his union and his political franchise to set against the power of ownership. Property in land on a large scale may represent a similar power over those who are forced to rent it for a livelihood. There are consequently forms of feudal land ownership in Europe, in some states of America and in the Orient, which are frequent sources of social injustice.

On the other hand property in land which does not extend beyond the capacity of one family to cultivate — the small freehold which determines a large part of the agriculture of the Western world — belongs to a unique category. The small freeholder may find it increasingly difficult to compete against mechanized large-scale production and to make a living without being overdriven. But on the other hand there is a special justification for this type of property, since it gives freedom to perform a social function without the interference of capricious power and without the exercise of power over others. Furthermore, there is a more organic relation between owner and property in agricultural land than in any type of industrial ownership. Small-scale property in industry and in retail trade possesses some of these same characteristics in a lesser degree. Yet there is always the danger that small-scale productive property, whether in land, industry or trade, may tempt the owner, in his competition with more powerful productive units, to exploit his own family and the other workers employed, especially since in any given case the latter may be too few to organize effectively.

(2) *The message of Christianity should throw a searchlight on the actual facts of the existing situation, and in particular reveal the human consequences of present forms of economic behavior.* It is this which saves statements of principles from being platitudes. The kind of critical analysis which is set forth in section two must be a part of the message of the church. Here it is important not to impute motives or to denounce individuals (except where special circumstances call for such denunciation) but to present facts in such a way that they speak for themselves to the individual conscience. What in isolation seems to be purely destructive criticism is a necessary part of the total process by which constructive change is brought about.

The most obvious human consequences of existing economic behavior are quite as much, if not more, within the province of the Christian as they are within the province of the expert in the social sciences. The clergyman in the course of pastoral work has opportunities, if he is capable of using them, of knowing what the present economic situation does to the character, the morale, the true welfare of men, women and children and to family life. The expert may have to supply statistics, but the meaning of the statistics can be known only to those who see the particular results of an economic situation in the lives of persons. As it has been said, " Love implies the ability to read statistics with compassion." Christian insight ought to enable men and women to see more deeply into the effects of an economic situation. Where there are secular agencies which have the facts, the task of the church is to aid in making those facts available to its members and especially to those who have a teaching function within the church. But there are occasions on which some agency of the church may have the task of securing the facts. This can be most helpful in controversial situations in which the church has a position of relative independence of the parties to the controversy.

It is not enough to catalogue particular cases of poverty and exploitation or to call attention to specific cases of selfish and irresponsible conduct on the part of those in power. It is the business of the church to point out where the economic institutions of our time are in themselves infected with evil. They place narrow limits on the choices of the best men who work within them. The individual employer, for example, is often greatly handicapped in paying a living wage if he must compete with less scrupulous employers. There are multitudes of high-minded Christians who as employers, businessmen and trade unionists do a great deal to develop happy relationships between

employers and employees and to preserve the highest standards of personal integrity within their spheres of influence.
Many of the most praiseworthy human motives — constructive service to mankind, the creation of cultural and
material values, the desire to achieve conditions essential
to the development of human personality — inspire their
conduct.   No criticisms of the present consequences of
economic behavior in general should obscure the positive
contribution of such men.   On the other hand the presence
of such conscientious Christians in places of responsibility
should not create the expectation that, without changes in
institutions and legal relationships, they will be able to
overcome the evils set forth in section three of this report.

(3) *This searchlight of the Christian message can also
make clear the obstacles to economic justice in the human
heart, and especially those that are present in the hearts of
people within the church.*   It is not enough that individual
Christians become good in their intentions or become
changed in their conscious motives.   What is needed is the
kind of self-knowledge which will help Christians to understand how far their attitudes are molded by the position
which they hold in the economic order.   Self-knowledge is
no less important than knowledge of external conditions,
and more important than the knowledge of the sins of
others.

Christians must come to understand how far they really
do seek, in spite of all pretensions to the contrary, a world
in which they and their group are on top, how far their
opinions on economic issues are controlled by the interests
of the group or class to which they belong, how far they
are deceived by false slogans and rationalizations, how far
they are callous to " evil at a distance " or to evil experienced by another national or class group than their own —
evil to which they may consent, for which they may vote,

or by which they may profit.   Here, again, the important activity is not to denounce, but to help people to that self-knowledge which comes from the perspective of the Christian emphasis upon sin, so that they will condemn themselves.

The various parts of the church must at this point be guided in the relative emphasis they place on different forms of self-deception by the character of their constituencies.   Those parts of the church which contain chiefly the comfortable middle classes should create an atmosphere in which it is most likely that the peculiarly middle class illusions will be punctured.   There is, for example, in these classes a tendency to take the present property system for granted and to regard as unjust changes which alter the present distribution of property or the present rights of owners.   The kind of Christian teaching about property which is outlined above is at this stage of special importance for these classes.

These classes must also come to see how onesided those conceptions of Christianity are which assume that because Christianity is a spiritual religion economic conditions do not greatly matter, or that it is enough to leave it to the grace of God to save souls in all varieties of external circumstances.   Justice may at this stage be embodied in the distribution of bread, but for that reason the quest for justice is not less spiritual.   Moreover, it is unseemly for people to be complacent in the face of existing obstacles to the personal development of others, obstacles which they have not themselves experienced.   To be complacent in this way because of a religious belief concerning the soul or God is to turn religion into an opiate for the conscience.

Also it is important in some countries that Christians in the comfortable middle classes be helped to realize that they are controlled by class interests quite as much as the workers or farmers, and that in some countries where organizations of workers and farmers are not far advanced they are themselves even more controlled by class interests than these other groups. The assumption that the interests of the middle classes are identical with the interests of the community is an illusion which unconsciously blinds many of the most sincere Christians and makes them unfair and self-righteous in their attitude toward those classes which at present are the chief sufferers from the economic order.

At the proper time and in the proper place the teaching of the church should also create an atmosphere in which the illusions of the working classes and other groups can readily be punctured. It is an illusion, for example, to suppose that the interests of the industrial workers are identical with those of the community.

What is important is that each group, in the most effective ways possible, be brought under the criticism which is implicit in Christian faith. In relationships between classes, we tend at present to see only the mote in our brother's eye. Christians have a special obligation, as they ought to have a special gift for this purpose, to try to interpret separate groups in society to one another. Barriers have to be broken through before they can be broken down. Self-sacrifice and compassion are good, but they are not, for example, what the poor today want of the well-to-do. Without the understanding mind which is able to think and feel the position of the other man, suspicion and distrust cannot be broken down. This power of delicate discernment and sensibility is rare in the world, because it is, in truth, a God-given grace and as such should be the peculiar contribution of the church to the making of true community.

Self-knowledge is a necessary condition for Christian repentance. The church should be able to bring about this condition of repentance because at the heart of its gospel it has a conception of human nature which should make men naturally suspicious of their own motives and which should thus lead them to put a strong burden of proof on themselves when their decisions coincide with their own economic advantage. In some cases it can also be said that the church (and this would mean especially the clergy) has some degree of detachment from the immediate pressure of the interests of economic groups and should be able to see the world from the point of view of more than one group. That this is true at present to only a small degree is itself one of the most tragic and sinful factors in the life of the church.

In the next decade those who are responsible for guiding the life of the church must seek, by means of these and other forms of teaching, to bring under moral control the attitude of their members in economic relationships — just as they have always sought to bring under moral control the attitude of their members in direct personal relationships. This task will involve far more than preaching. It must become an integral part of the whole life and atmosphere of the church. The church as a worshiping community must relate its acts of repentance and dedication to the economic order in which its members live. Emphasis must here be placed upon the importance of teaching children and young people before the crusts formed by class and convention close their minds. The training of the clergy must include preparation for this kind of teaching.

In concluding this part of the report, we wish to emphasize that the work of teaching to which we have drawn attention above cannot be performed without the cooperation of the laity. Groups of men and women who are responsible for the conduct of industry and the functioning of the economic order must be helped to discover for themselves how the principles which we have tried to enunciate can be worked out in the spheres of life which are in some measure under their control. This opens up a large field for experiment and calls for fresh developments in many directions as well as for new types of ministry.

6. IMMEDIATE CHRISTIAN ACTION

(1) Action by the Churches

(a) *Reform of Their Own Institutional Life*. It is within the power of the churches to set their own houses in order where this requires to be done. As an economic and social organization a church, be it local, national or ecumenical, cannot escape in sharing in some measure the features of the secular society in which it is rooted, but in so far as its members are sensitive to the spirit of Christ they will be critically aware of that relationship. A church which is prophetic and apostolic, as the Christian fellowship is meant to be, will live under a divine compulsion to realize the perfection of God, as completely as human imperfection will allow, in every concrete situation of its life — and having done all, its members will know themselves to be " unprofitable servants." A church, moreover, is not likely to convince men in an economic-minded age that it is a supernatural society if it allows its economic and social organization to remain sub-worldly. In regard to the sources of income, methods of raising money and administration of property, as well as in the terms on which it employs men and women and their tenure of office, churches ought to be scrupulous to avoid the evils that Christians deplore in secular society.

Moreover, the economic organization of the church ought to help and not hinder the comity in Christ which should be the feature of its common life. There should, therefore, be a reasonable uniformity in the payment of those who hold the same spiritual office and they ought to be paid according to the real needs of themselves and their families, and sufficiently to allow them to give themselves, without too great anxiety concerning daily bread, to their spiritual service. It is not tolerable that those who minister to the rich should be comparatively well off and those who minister to the poor should be poor for that reason alone. It is not right that those who have greater responsibility in the church or greater gifts of utterance than their brethren should for that reason alone have much larger incomes. It does not express Christian solidarity that churches in poor and depressing districts should be handicapped by an inefficient and unlovely plant, which would not be tolerated in the assemblies of the rich. So long as the institution has these defects in its organization, it will corrupt most subtly the vocational sense of its ministry and prejudice its witness in the world. On the other hand, if its members were more continuously critical of its economic structure and were quick to reform evils in it, such concrete action would release spiritual power.

(b) *Development of New Machinery for Research and Action.* Hitherto the churches have been only partially informed and sporadically articulate on the subjects dealt with in this report. Although churches as such have no special competence in the technical sphere, yet it is in and through the technical sphere that spiritual principles have to find expression. In the words of Baron von Hügel, " the supernatural is known in and through the natural."

Before truthful judgment can be made or principles successfully applied in concrete situations, the relevant facts, material and personal, require to be studied and mastered. To this end the churches ought — where they are not already equipped for the purpose — to have at their service, regionally as well as ecumenically, organs both for study and research, as well as for witness and action in appropriate circumstances. Only so far as these are first-rate in competence and equipment are they likely to command attention within and without the churches.

In the past, pronouncements sometimes and preachings often have failed to carry weight because the speakers assumed a technical knowledge which they did not have. We would urge, therefore, that in the forming of Christian opinion there should be more cooperation between clergy and ministers on the one hand, and on the other those of the laity who are engaged in industry, commerce and public administration.

(c) *Integration of Work and Worship.* One of the tasks laid upon the church, which is not easy to carry out in the existing state of things, is to re-establish in the experience of men and women a unity of work and worship. While their irrelevance to each other at the present time is partly because much work is pagan and unworshipful, it is also due to the fact that the daily business of the modern world, and the problems and issues dealt with in this report, are not sufficiently woven into the liturgy and worship of the church. Unless men are required to ask forgiveness, to make petition and to give thanks for the things with which they are chiefly concerned day by day, public worship will begin to seem secondary. There should be no discontinuity between the sanctuary and the life and work in office, factory or home, for the God we worship cares for the whole of men's lives and not only for that part of life which is specifically religious.

(2) Action by Christians

(a) *Action within the Existing Economic Order.* Whatever their reaction to the existing situation, Christians are under constraint to carry their faith and loyalty into con-

crete situations, the daily business and the personal relationships of their life. In the integrity and faithfulness
which they bring to " the daily round and common task,"
they may be instruments, in some measure, of the creative
work and the justice and mercy of God. Outside the fields
of business, industry and the professions there are, moreover, varied opportunities for Christian service. The increasing amount of law and legislation which controls industrial activity and social life in the modern state depends
for its administration and good results upon the actions of
associations of employers, trade unions, government of-
ficials and social workers, both paid and voluntary. The
development of national and local government and of the
cooperative movements provide large fields for social action
and fellowship which the Christian should be anxious to
enter.

(b) *Group Experiments.* Because some things cannot
be changed without state action or international adjustment, the effective power of " two or three " men of conviction who make themselves into a Christian " cell " must
not be underestimated. In fact, the world over there are
such groups who in the spirit of him who walked the second
mile are proving what can be done to bridge unbridgeable
gulfs and to bring back into society those who have felt
themselves to be outcast and unwanted.

(c) *Changing the Economic Order.* Finally, in accordance with the argument developed in section four of this
report, Christians have a particular responsibility to make
whatever contribution they can toward the transformation,
and if necessary the thorough reconstruction, of the present
economic and political system, through their membership
in political parties, trade unions, employers' organizations
and other groups. In this part of their Christian duty, the
same characteristics are called for, though in a different

form, as those which Christians are called on to show in all their other activities: readiness to make sacrifices, to take effective action, to forgive those that trespass against them and to love those that seem to be their enemies.

Christianity sincerely professed brings to those who are striving for a better order of society the serene confidence that to them that love God, all things work together for good. This world is God's world. His Spirit is alive today as yesterday. Here in his own good time his kingdom will come. If men will put themselves unreservedly and humbly at the service of God, he is able to overrule their stupidity and sin and to use them to set forward his purpose for mankind, which is a society better than their deserving as it is beyond their desires.

IV. REPORT OF THE SECTION ON CHURCH, COMMUNITY AND STATE IN RELATION TO EDUCATION *

1. INTRODUCTION

Education is the process by which the community seeks to open its life to all the individuals within it and enable them to take their part in it. It attempts to pass on to them its culture, including the standards by which it would have them live. Where that culture is regarded as final, the attempt is made to impose it on younger minds. Where it is viewed as a stage in a development, younger minds are trained both to receive it and to criticize and improve upon it. This culture is composed of various elements. It runs from rudimentary skill and knowledge up to the interpretations of the universe and of man by which the community lives. It is not the purpose of this report to deal with the problem either of education in general or of religious education, but rather of the relation between them. As secular systems to an increasing extent claim to determine the inner life of men it becomes difficult to draw a sharp distinction between the religious and the nonreligious elements in education. Here we are principally concerned

* This report was submitted substantially in its present form to the conference on the last day of its meeting. The conference received the report, referred it back to the section for revision in the light of the discussion, and commended it to the serious and favorable consideration of the churches. Before being submitted to the conference the report was approved by the section. One or two members of the section expressed reservations in regard to particular points but did not oppose the adoption of the report. After the discussion in the plenary session, the report was revised by the drafting committee of the section, which made a few minor changes but none of substance.

69

with the problem of the respective spheres and mutual relations of church, community and state in so far as they may
be educating or may claim the right to educate the same
persons.

2. CHURCH, COMMUNITY AND STATE IN EDUCATION

Before we consider these relations we must set forth certain characteristics of church, community and state which
affect the problem.

(1) The Church

By the church we mean in this report the fellowship of
Christians organized in the existing churches.[1] Her gospel
claims the whole man, spirit, mind and body, and every
human institution for the service of God. Nothing which
affects man's individual or social life is a matter of indifference to her. She is concerned that every child and adult
shall receive the fullest education consistent with his capacities; but she must make plain that no education is adequate without the living encounter with God and the response of personal faith. It is not her province as an
organized institution to assume responsibility for the entire
conduct of life and education. She recognizes the functions of the home, the community and the state in education and lays upon her members their obligation to work
within those realms, even where she carries on education
through schools of her own.

The church has in mind God's will for her — a will never
fully achieved but to which she must always seek to conform. Her members have to confess with penitence that
they have frequently failed to understand and obey that
will.

[1] In our use of the term " the church " throughout the report, we do
not refer to the whole body of Christ in the mystical sense.

(a) *The Church a Fellowship of Free Persons under Law to Christ.* The church is a fellowship of persons freed by the spirit of Christ. She reveres personality, since man is created in God's image and God has revealed himself through men responsive to his Spirit, and his Word became flesh in Jesus Christ.

She should be opposed to an education which teaches men to subordinate themselves to any human force as the final authority — be it the will of the majority, or of a leader or of an absolute state. That is to violate the sanctity of conscience which must be kept responsible to God alone. In her teaching, governments exist for men, not men for governments. Every human being has unique worth as a child of God, and should be so educated as to encourage him to make his singular contribution to the commonweal.

She should be equally opposed to any system which stimulates the unconditional self-expression of the individual. She ought to insist upon the obligations of fellowship and to set the areas of obligation about the individual in concentric circles — his home, his neighborhood, his country, his world. She must learn afresh the importance of the organic relationships in which God has placed us in making us members one of another. This is her spiritual basis for social solidarity. On this foundation education in obedience to the law of Christian love creates consciences which cohere and form a stable society. Such education produces that spiritual discipline without which nations disintegrate.

(b) *The Church a Redemptive Fellowship.* The church is a redemptive and sanctifying fellowship. The Christian presupposition is that all men are sinners and that the culture of any community or nation is a mixture of good and evil elements. The church's chief concern is to bring every child and adult under the control of a transforming Master, Jesus Christ, and to train him to receive the culture of his community with spiritual discrimination acquired by viewing it in the light of Christ. A product of Christian education is therefore both a grateful recipient of and a critic of the cultural heritage. He is a patriot, but a discerning patriot. It is this dual attitude, both appreciative and critical, toward the national life and institutions which it is the aim of the church's education to develop. In some quarters this is regarded as the church's offense against the community.

(c) *The Church a Supra-national Fellowship.* The church is a supra-national fellowship. She draws her members from all nations and believes that they have more in common with one another than they have with non-Christian fellow citizens, inasmuch as Christ and the Christian heritage are of greater worth than is any national inheritance apart from him. She inculcates loyalty to God above loyalty to the state, and places fidelity to the Christian fellowship above fidelity to the nation. Where she is true to her nature she cannot allow national interests to be set before those of humanity, nor permit any people to fancy that it can develop its national life without a just regard for every other people. She must educate her people to consider themselves as belonging first to God and to his church and secondarily to their nation.

(d) *The Church a Supra-racial Fellowship.* The church is a supra-racial fellowship. She embraces in her Christian brotherhood men of every blood and color. While she cannot be blind to the fact that all races are not equally advanced, she teaches their equal worth before him who is the Father of them all. Nor can she compute the relative value to humanity of the diverse racial characteristics. If she be true to her gospel, she is compelled to protest against injurious discriminations by those of one race against those of another. When a state in its laws or a community in its customs enacts the dominance of the inhabitants of one stock and accords those of other races an inferior status, there clearly ought to be a conflict in education between church and state or church and community.

(e) *The Church a Supra-class Fellowship.* The church is a supra-class fellowship. In her membership there should be no place for social distinctions. In fact she has often been false to her principles and has become associated with a class or classes in the community. But she is concerned with men not as economic men but as children of God. By that interest in them she is committed to stand for such social justice as makes possible for all the inhabitants of every land a physical and intellectual life worthy of sons and daughters of the Most High and levels barriers which hinder them from living together in spiritual comradeship. She cannot tolerate social distinctions which breed insolence in some and servility in others. Nor can she commit herself to the interests of any one class. So where a state is dominated, as is often the case, by one or more economic groups, and is attempting in its education to perpetuate an aristocratic or a bourgeois or a proletarian culture, there will be differences between church and state. The church, as the representative of a loving God, must be especially concerned with those groups in the community which are least privileged and labor to obtain for them a just share in the national heritage. Where the community denies to some children an education which would enable them to develop their full power, or where it permits their exploitation in industry, the church in God's name must enter the lists as their protector.

(f) *The Church an Eternal Fellowship.* The church is an eternal fellowship. She views men not only as citizens for a brief span of years in an earthly community and state, but also as those who are called to be citizens of the abiding city of God. This does not mean a lack of interest in their earthly lives. On the contrary, these assume a new meaning as a preliminary education for an immortal destiny. No training which fits only for useful citizenship in some community on earth seems to her to do justice to human beings, who are not creatures of time, but children of God, intended for eternal life with him in a spiritual commonwealth.

The church claims to be all these things. But the church cannot substantiate her claim because she can neither speak nor act as one universal community. This gravely affects her capacity to discharge her own particular function in education; it weakens her appeals to youth and renders her less able either to arrive at a satisfactory and harmonious agreement with the state, when friendly, or to resist its encroachments, when hostile. Until we have set our own house in order in this matter of unity, we shall not be able fully to meet our responsibility to either the state, the community or the world. In the progress toward this union each church should acquaint her own members with the life and work of other communions and with the work of the ecumenical movement.

The educational mission of the church is interpreted in different senses. To some it is essentially distinct from the general education provided by any secular community. Thus Christian education can never be treated as a special case of general education. The interest of the church in education as in other spheres must always be seen over against that of nation or state. Her real concern is with regeneration, which can never come about as the result of a process of development but is an act of God.

To others regeneration is indeed primary, but there are

other considerations which the church must have in view. Therefore her educational task is twofold: First, she has a share in the education of the whole man, body, mind and spirit. The God of grace is also the God of nature and of history. Man may know and serve him in every activity of life. Here the church can cooperate with the community to a considerable extent. Second, the church is also engaged in education in so far as she uses educational method in imparting the content of Christian truth, developing the spirit and habit of worship and bringing men to share in the active life of the Christian fellowship. These differences of approach and emphasis affect our conception of the educational mission of the church and are to be understood even where they are not explicitly stated.

(2) The State

The state is concerned with the intelligence of its people, for upon their abilities in agriculture and industry and commerce depend its economic welfare and its national strength. It has an interest in forming the minds of its people so that they support the national institutions and cooperate with the undertakings of its rulers. Its purpose is to educate a people to be loyal and capable citizens or subjects, devoted with soul and mind and strength to their nation. It usually seeks to provide at least the minimum education for all and to open further opportunities of learning to the talented.

Every state is obliged to maintain national solidarity. In an era of social disintegration, it is not surprising that certain states have taken special measures to re-establish and maintain the unity of their people. Their governments seek to control all the agencies which influence human belief and behavior. They wish to use the school system, the press, broadcasting, the cinema and the theater for the purpose of inculcating their ideals and fashioning the type of citizens they desire.

Others which place more emphasis upon freedom recognize the rights of various agencies to share in the task of education. Such states regard their culture as a stage in a development and do not impose it rigidly upon the minds of their youth. They wish their cultures to be enriched by the contributions of creative citizens and place fewest restrictions upon the pursuit and discussion of truth. They would have their schools produce a citizenry of the present type but also individuals who transcend that type. They recognize that those who go beyond it are factors in social change and may be leaders in national progress.

(3) The Community

The community in its forms of life largely molds the personalities of its members. The system of relationships — social, economic and political — is a more potent educational influence than any formal schooling. Christian education is deeply concerned, therefore, with shaping the patterns of community life in a way that will foster Christian insights and conduct.

In some lands the community carries on education through institutions of learning which are officially under neither church nor state control. These schools and colleges had their counterparts in the medieval universities, which originally were confederations of scholars closely related to the church, but with a measure of freedom from ecclesiastical authority and from government supervision. Such institutions today provide varieties of education and make distinctive contributions to the national life. In them truths and values not yet generally accepted, or out of fashion, may be developed and conserved. They can carry on their work uncramped by the standardization

which government authorities usually impose or by the
restrictions frequently set by church authorities. The state
lays down certain requirements as to the extent of the education which they offer before it recognizes them as substi-
tutes for its own governmentally controlled institutions of
learning. It may assist them with grants or by exempting
their property from taxation. They may be allies of the
church in furnishing religious education, although not
under any denominational oversight. The varieties of
schools and colleges through which culture is given to the
oncoming generation add to the national spiritual wealth.
The church has an interest in institutions of learning both
because of the enrichment they may bring to the mind of a
nation and because she is enabled to establish schools of
her own for the training of her leaders and thus provide a
type of education not supplied by the government institutions.

3. FACTORS IN THE PRESENT SITUATION

There are circumstances in the life of our time which
complicate the relations of church, community and state in
education and occasion conflicts between them. Among
these we call attention to the following:

(a) *Secularization of Modern Life.* The outstanding
characteristic of our world is the general secularization of
life and thought. The presuppositions and motives of both
private and public conduct have become exclusively this-
worldly. In some lands there is an open break with religion in all its forms. Elsewhere we are witnessing the
re-emergence of pagan types of religion, which make a
mundane good, such as the race or the nation, the supreme
object of man's loyalty. And in every country there are
subtle influences of community sentiment and of daily practice which deny or ignore the Christian meaning of life.

(b) *Faith in Man's Power to Direct his Destiny*. The rapid advance in the sciences and in the development of machinery have brought men to trust in their own abilities. Whole peoples have substituted for their former religion a confidence in man's collective power to create a world after his heart's desire. Psychology in particular has developed methods and techniques for handling spiritual difficulties. Parents and teachers turn increasingly to child-guidance clinics for assistance in dealing with the moral problems of children. A growing number of adults seek the advice of psychotherapists in their perplexities and troubles, and deem this a satisfactory substitute for the direction once sought in the church's ministry. The teaching profession has learned much from psychology, and not a few teachers are imbued with the confidence that a well developed secular educational system can fully prepare its pupils for life. Unhappily the churches have not always been awake or hospitable to the new knowledge and have thus widened the breach between themselves and the representatives of the sciences.

(c) *Social Disintegration*. A second phenomenon characteristic of our time is social disintegration. Its effects are most clearly seen where the advent of modern civilization disrupts a primitive society. But in many countries industrialization and urbanization have tended to destroy the bonds which formerly linked men in their communal life. In place of membership in a social group with recognized obligations, men have become irresponsible individuals or have developed a new mass consciousness. This is as true of the Christian church as it is of society as a whole. Moreover the commonly accepted religious convictions and generally acknowledged ethical ideals which lent support to the growing personality have given place in some lands to a widespread skepticism and relativism and elsewhere to an uncritical obedience to exclusive group loyalties.

(d) *The Weakening of Family Ties.* A most serious feature of the tendency to social disintegration is the weakening of the institution of the home. The family has always been regarded as the principal agency in the Christian nurture of the young. The impermanence of marital ties in some lands, the effect of modern industry in taking both parents out of the home in many places, the appalling blight upon family life of unemployment or casual employment, under other circumstances, have led to the decay of the influences of the home. Even in nominally Christian homes we cannot now take a religious background for granted. This confronts the church with a new problem in its own fellowship.

(e) *The Shift of Interest in Education.* A fundamental change in the aims and practice of education is the steady movement of the interest of educators from the knowledge and skill which their pupils acquire to the pupils themselves. Until recent times much public education has confined itself to instruction in certain subjects and has regarded the training of character as the function of the church. Today, however, it is setting out to create a particular kind of person in accordance with its interpretation of the ends of man's existence. This interpretation even at its best does not admit the full claims of Christianity and the church therefore should be aware of the difference between such an interpretation and her own.

(f) *New Educational Agencies.* New means of public education are now in operation which are profoundly affecting men's minds. Broadcasting and the cinema provide unprecedented opportunities for reaching and influencing masses of the population. The uses to which these

new means are put may promote propaganda and distort
values at the expense of true education and may cause
friction between the various institutions concerned with
education.

(g) *The Increasing Intervention of the State in Education.*   There has been an increasing intervention of the
state in all departments of life.   It was accelerated after the
war, when the state alone seemed strong enough to control
the events of the economic and social crisis.   This intervention spread over all areas of the national life, including
education.   The result has been tension between the state
and other factors in education — the home, the community
and the church.   Certain governments have taken exclusive
control of the organizations of youth, in particular those
concerned with sport, so important in the eyes of young
people.   In the social disintegration it has been the state
which has marshaled the new educational agencies for the
fulfillment of its purposes.   And it is in the state that man's
confidence in himself has come to fullest expression.

4. CRUCIAL ISSUES FOR CHRISTIANS IN EDUCATION

In the present situation there are four major issues on
which church and state conflict in education.

(a) *Freedom.*   One is the issue of freedom.   For any
education worthy of the name truth is supreme and there
must be freedom both to seek and to teach it.   This is very
different from political propaganda which denies that freedom.   Christians in every country should endeavor to understand the distinction.   In reaction to ideas dominant in
recent times, there are powerful movements in education
which subordinate the individual to the interests of the
community as these are understood by the political authority.   The attempt is made to conform him to a sharply defined pattern, and deviations from the desired type are no

tolerated. It must be recognized that even under these systems the individual may find both release and discipline in a wholehearted response to the claims of nation or community or class. But such systems have not solved the problem of how to secure conformity and produce creative types of personality. The church's quarrel with them is that their patterns are sub-Christian, and sometimes anti-Christian, and their rigidity cramps the growth of children of God. It is her conviction that the proper correction of error is not the use of repression but the appeal to larger truth. Education must encourage a disciplined sense of obligation and the unfettered development of the individual's capacities.

It is the church's aim, as has been shown, to educate free persons under law to Christ. In her view, however, freedom is not a natural gift. At this point much educational theory is unrealistic, ignoring the necessity for inward deliverance and unity. The freedom she seeks is both liberty from the tyranny and deceit of evil passions within the heart, and strength of character to preserve liberty of conscience amid external pressure. It is her conviction that personality attains this freedom and completeness only in obedience to God. Such spiritual freedom has been attained by Christians even under most adverse outward circumstances. Nevertheless, service to God demands the service of one's fellow men and the obtaining for them of external conditions favorable to their fullest life.

(b) *Social Disintegration*. In the face of social disintegration, the community is animated by a resolve to restore organic unity in the national life. Because of Christianity's development of a fellowship which overleaps barriers of nation and race and class and sets Christians in an eternal as well as in the temporal order, the church is looked on as a hostile force. In the field of education the effort is made to banish everything which conflicts with a common national ethos. This is true not only in totalitarian states, but also in democracies where educators regard Christian faith with its distinctive fellowship as divisive of the community, and would therefore accord it no place in that education for the social order which they envisage.

It must be asserted that Christianity is opposed to any deification of the community or state. These can never be supreme objects of loyalty or the ultimate social goals. Christianity broke up the community-state-church in the ancient world where religion was merely one aspect of the communal life. It introduced a new principle by inculcating a double loyalty — to Caesar and to God. But Christians recognize the values in national life and culture. They acknowledge that the state, like the family, has its claims upon a man. Civic duty involves his loyal obedience to all that the state demands of him, in so far as it does not conflict with his loyalty to God. Moreover, such loyalty to God brings into society a principle of redemption and of growth. To see all things in the light of the absolute claims of God is to bring to bear on them a searching criticism and to subject them to a transforming judgment.

The church must penitently confess that, while on mission fields there is a sharp differentiation between the ideals in her education and those of the community, in so-called Christian lands the Christian understanding of the way of life is often not distinctive from that generally accepted. The church herself has too readily compromised and her witness loses its pungency. The contemporary pressure of aggressive non-Christian systems must be viewed as one of God's methods of recalling her to a fresh discovery of the truths and ideals of which she is the trustee.

(c) *Control of Youth Movements.* One of the characteristic features of our time is the response made by youth

to the appeal of political leaders who offer them a part in
the building of a nation. There has followed in some states
a control of youth organizations so exclusive that church,
family and community have been deprived of their due
share in the full development of the new generation. But
we must recognize that there is something in the totalitarian claim that captivates contemporary youth. There are
a sense of community, definiteness of purpose and demand
upon the whole energies and devotion of the personality.
This is a challenge to the church to present Jesus Christ to
the youth of every land as Lord and to enlist their devotion
for his purpose for mankind through the community of his
church.

(d) *Modern Knowledge, Method and Technique.* Both
state and community in their education are making use of
the new knowledge and agencies referred to in the preced-
ing section. This has brought them into those fields of
character and spiritual health which the church has regarded as peculiarly her own. She must welcome an education which concerns itself with the whole man, and new
sciences and techniques which assist in the solution of spiritual difficulties. It is increasingly apparent that she cannot rest satisfied with the education of the intellect alone.
She must address herself to the infinitely more difficult tasks
of preventing and removing those emotional biases which
in most men dull the voice of conscience, and of exposing
the rationalizations under which they cloak their selfishness, their love of power and the cowardice of their hearts.

The church ought to make clear, not only to the community and the state but also to her own members, that the
complexity of modern life has strengthened the tendency
to overestimate professional and social success and the
means of achieving it. Under pressure of anxiety lest
young people fail to find secure foothold in industrial, com-

mercial or professional life parents have come to attach overwhelming importance to the acquirement of vocational or academic qualifications for employment. The power of truly sensitive response to the world of nature and of art and to the qualities and claims of other members of the human family is not developed as it should be, nor is insight into the meaning and purpose of life as a whole. And here also the church must penitently confess that not only a secularized community and state but even her own members often forget that strength and serenity of soul, the result of faith in God, are more indispensable than economic security or professional success.

The situation makes upon her a double demand. In the first place, she must see to it that those who engage in her work are aware of the aid which modern knowledge can give in the education of both old and young and can turn that aid to account. They must know what is being done in these fields that they may direct such as need this help to those competent to supply it. Further, the church must keep her own education abreast of the improvements which these sciences have brought to general educational theory and practice. But no technique alone will suffice for the end of the building up of the whole man into Christ. The spirit of Christ must be mediated through persons to persons. The church must proclaim in its purity her own essential gospel of the healing mercy of Christ; she must proclaim with power that through the appropriation of this mercy men receive salvation of soul and that apart from it there can be no final attainment of mental and spiritual health.

5. THE IMMEDIATE TASKS OF THE CHURCH IN EDUCATION

While the church in some parts of the world finds herself hampered by restraints upon her liberties, almost everywhere she is not making full use of the freedom accorded her. We would attempt to set before ourselves and our brethren in all the churches the tasks in education to which we should address ourselves. In considering them we discover that an impediment more serious than any restriction from without is the disunion of the church's own forces. Sometimes where educational leaders in community and state are eager to cooperate with her they are perplexed by the differing proposals of her various communions and embarrassed by the rivalries among them. They hesitate also to involve public institutions in sectarian strife. Unquestionably there is a basic unity among the vast majority of Christians in their spiritual interpretation of the universe and of man and in their consequent ethic. Yet nothing seems harder than to express it without antagonizing Christians who wish more included in the statement of it or wish a different emphasis in what is said. It is the lack of a common mind on the fundamentals of Christian faith and life which has even pushed some states, where those in authority were themselves Christians, into secularist systems of education. If the church is to discharge her teaching duty she must bring her communions into a common front on educational issues and unite her forces in fulfilling this urgent task.

(a) *A Theology Relevant to Current Life.* Christian faith has always formulated itself to meet current errors and to win the contemporary mind. Confronted with secularism and aggressive non-Christian systems of thought and conduct, the church finds many of her loyal adherents in the teaching profession, as well as in the mass of her members, confused as to the meaning of the gospel and the principles by which it would have men live in the present world. As we have pointed out, the attempt to reach a common mind on the fundamentals of Christian faith and conduct to be taught has often failed. But the urgency of the crisis in which we find ourselves and the necessity of much greater unity among Christians, if the church is to cooperate with the state and community in education, impel us in this ecumenical conference to make an attempt to sum up basic assumptions which underlie an education acceptable to Christians.

Christians share the conviction that there is one living and true God, Creator and Lord of earth and heaven, whose universe is planned and controlled by wisdom and love, and the chief of whose creatures is man, possessed of reason and conscience, and capable of becoming like him in character and sharing eternal life with him in an enduring society of the righteous. But Christians know themselves and all men as sinners and members of a race estranged from God in pride and at war within itself through selfishness. Man, both individually and collectively, needs redemption. God, the Creator and Lord, is also the Redeemer revealed in Christ, who died and rose again for us. God gives himself in his Spirit to re-create individuals and communities who turn to him in repentance and to guide them to discover for themselves the way of Christ and to grow into his stature in faith and hope and love.

The divine purpose to redeem, which is eternal in the will of God, was disclosed in the series of historic divine acts by which the purpose was realized in the life of man. The story of the revelation of this purpose and of its fulfillment, together with an inspiring record of the long history of the people of God — first as the Jewish church, inchoate, provisional, expectant, then divinely established as the body of Christ — is told in the Bible. To this we continually appeal. It is our charter, the main evidence for our belief that the heavens have been opened and that God is a God who lives and acts. The Bible has not always been wisely used, but the survival of Christianity will depend, as it has always depended, on its continual use. Because it comes from God the Bible has a universal quality, and by it man is judged. There is in the Bible the true revelation of the nature of God to men of every age, authenticated alike by the authority of the church and by the interior witness of the Spirit in the heart of man; there is an interpretation of human history; there is a view of life, which can be obtained from no other quarter. The Bible has that to say about God and about man which the present generation, perhaps more than any other, needs urgently to hear.

This understanding of God and of man needs to be expressed in a living theology which grows out of the devotion of multitudes of Christian people and out of the collaboration of Christian thinkers in all countries and in all communions of the church. In particular it needs to be embodied in the minds and lives of Christians in the teaching profession, who by their example and by their interpretation of the culture they impart communicate their faith.

In the work of education some would stress the fact that the gospel must appear irrational to those whose initial assumptions are not Christian. Others would rather emphasize that reason is the gift of God whereby we understand his message and that we should be ready to give a reason to others for the hope that is in us; the Christian church, they would say, is one of the strongholds of belief in reason in a world that seems to be more and more emotionally controlled. Both views are alike in acknowledging that the gospel is supra-rational. Both agree that it is part of Christian duty to educate the power of criticism so that people may discriminate between those elements in the thought and movement of our time which are God's gift and those which are incompatible with the Christian understanding of life. Yet there is here a real difference in emphasis such as was referred to in section three of this report.

(b) *A Philosophy and a Psychology of Education.* There is also need to formulate a philosophy of education from the Christian standpoint and to develop a psychology which does not disregard the significance of religious experience but finds in man's relationship with God the supreme integrating and directing power in human personality. When we ask ourselves so apparently simple a question as why children should go to school and what purpose teachers have in teaching them we raise greater issues than perhaps we realize. The relation of religion to education cannot be made clear if education is a series of uncoordinated studies and activities. We cannot discern the significance and the aim of the whole if we have not considered the relative value and the interdependence of the various parts of the curriculum, to say nothing of all that makes up school life. Again, the very basis of our faith is the self-revelation of God in Jesus Christ, who for us men and for our salvation was made man. So we lose much if we do not try to understand the characteristics of human nature and its growth toward the complete man.

(c) *The Educational Task of the Church in her own Institutions and through her own Membership.* It has already been said that the patterns of community life have a more potent educational influence than any formal schooling. We therefore consider first those members of the church whose task it is to foster the growth of Christian personality in the various forms and relationships found within the community.

Of these the most fundamental is the home. All mothers and fathers ought to be made aware that their way of life is more influential during the infancy of their children than any oral teaching later on. Deep-seated emotional tendencies and moral attitudes are engendered in the earliest years of a child's life by its daily experience of sympathy and love or antagonism and fear in its simplest and most necessary relationships with its father and mother. The first introduction to worship and to the Bible should be given, wherever possible, by the parents. We need to remember that parents cannot accomplish this task satisfactorily without preparation and help. The work of parent education through voluntary organizations is a powerful agency or ally of the church.

The personal impressions made on the pupils by their contact with the teacher and with one another in the school are more indelible and pervasive than the effects of formal instruction. Therefore the church has a paramount responsibility regarding the supply, training and continuous encouragement of Christian teachers. Where she has teacher-training colleges under her own control she may influence the whole tone of education not only in church schools but also in those of the state. Even where this opportunity is not given she may render a service of incalculable importance by helping teachers, through their membership in the church and through voluntary associations, to maintain their spiritual vigor and purpose as teachers. In two directions particularly the church can help the teaching profession. The first is the understanding and choice of biblical material, the elucidation of the central doctrines of the Christian faith and the discussion of special difficulties in dealing with these. The second is an understanding of the nature of worship, and practice in leading children's worship; for no matter how successful a teacher may be in imparting the facts of the Christian revelation, the child's religious life cannot develop as it should unless worship is central in it.

It remains true as it has always been that the factor of

supreme importance in Sunday school work is the teacher's own Christian experience and love of children. But if the effect of this attitude is not to be lost and if the decline in attendance in certain countries is to be arrested, teachers must be encouraged and helped to equip themselves as fully as possible both in knowledge of the Bible and of the church's life and activities, and in the understanding of how children grow and learn. The church should be willing to utilize in her Sunday school organization and methods the best educational knowledge and experience available, and thus encourage the participation in Sunday school work of trained teachers and of young people who ought to use the advantages of their own higher education in her service.

We have been discussing the preparation of teachers for giving religious instruction; but the teacher's whole outlook will influence the pupil's interpretation of all that he learns. As regards so-called secular subjects we must remember that, especially in secondary schools, colleges and universities, disciplines such as history and biology handled in a purely secular way, without so much as a glance in the direction of the God of history and of nature, may exert a negative influence more powerful than any number of courses in religion. On the other hand, courses in religious knowledge should be given so that the pupil faces the realities of personal and community life. One great cause of secularization is the fact that religious teaching has been given in a way which seems to indicate that there is a necessary clash between scientific knowledge and the biblical view of God, man and nature. Without trying in the least to give " scientific " proof for what can be known only by revelation, the teaching of religion should avoid at all costs bringing young people into a false dilemma. They should never feel that they have to choose between what they take to be the voice of the church and the call of truth.

Without a lay leadership which combines intellectual ability with vital Christian experience, the church cannot effectively present her message either in the schools and universities or within her own fellowship. At present the development of such leadership is seriously curtailed by the secularization of many colleges and universities which were founded on a Christian basis. This situation has many causes, such as the frequent exclusion of religious knowledge from the curriculum, inadequate concern for Christian personality in the selection of members of staff, and pressure of academic and extra-curricular activities which leave little room for corporate worship. The years spent at school or college may where there is a chapel lead to an attachment to the worship and fellowship then experienced and to an estrangement from the worship and fellowship of a congregation. This separation may even lead to a complete detachment from organized religion. These difficulties can be overcome only through the presentation of the Christian gospel in terms of thought and action related to the experience of young people and through a determined and discerning effort to enlist them, when they leave school and college, in great enterprises of a social and missionary character. Voluntary Christian associations in the colleges and universities provide an ecumenical fellowship and can be used to link up students with the local church.

The church cannot but be concerned with the youth movements which play so large a part in the life of the world today. Leadership will belong to those who understand youth's capacity for unselfish devotion and obedience and its desire for a life in comradeship. It is the church's responsibility to see that those of her young people who excel in leadership and capacity recognize the possibilities of Christian service in these movements. This involves not only a personal faith in and loyalty to Christ but also personal discipline and a constant study of the meaning of the gospel and its application in the world today.

The church's ministry of teaching is wider than that of school and college. Adult education is not a matter of overtaking deficiencies due to neglect in childhood and youth. It is the continuing process of growth in Christian character and understanding. The members of the church need much clearer and more systematic teaching of Christian truth and its implications for conduct. Ignorance of what the Christian faith is and of the obligations which it imposes is widespread and alarming particularly among young people. Still more so is the degree to which her members fail to take seriously in their business and civic and other social relations the Christian loyalty which they acknowledge. The majority of them seem pathetically ignorant of the Christian way and of the resources for following it to be had in that communion with God which is the life of the church. Preaching needs to be supplemented by a full and carefully planned program of Christian education in every parish or congregation. Much help can be obtained by making use of the facilities provided by recognized adult educational organizations, universities and others. Groups of persons, moreover, with common responsibilities in the family, in business, in industry, in trade or profession should be encouraged to seek together the Christian solution of their problems and the further advances that they can make in discharging their duties. Church leaders must work out means of utilizing the press, broadcasting and the cinema in the Christian education both of their own people and of the community at large.

Many of the studies described in the foregoing paragraphs can be pursued only in leisure time. But health of mind and spirit no less than health of body can be secured only if there is due enjoyment in that leisure of recreative activities also, such as sports and pastimes, music and the plastic arts, literature and the drama, travel and exploration of the countryside. The church, as well as the state and the community, may contribute to the provision of facilities for these pursuits. She must do what she can to educate her own people in the meaning and use of leisure. She should also help to spread throughout the community a sense of its obligations regarding both the adequacy and the standards of the opportunities for the wholesome employment of leisure offered to all its members.

But with the enormous increase in unemployment during recent years, leisure time has become one of the most serious educational problems. The immense strides in technology in both industry and agriculture and the growing disparity between production and consumption have brought about a condition of unemployment which threatens to become permanent. Even in socially normal times substantial portions of our population are without work. Furthermore, the shortening of the working day is adding to the leisure time of the regularly employed.

The educational implications of these facts are large and serious. The cultural and spiritual wants of men far outrun their material needs. Yet progress in the cultural and spiritual realm lags far behind material progress through discovery and invention. This is one of the main causes for the social disintegration to which reference has been made. The new leisure presents an opportunity for adult education on a large scale which Christians are called upon to promote, and for adult Christian education in which the church should actively participate.

Since education is a part of the church's mission, teaching is a function of her ministry in which the ordained minister and the lay teacher are partners. Each brings to the common task the fruits of a distinctive training and experience and each has much to learn from the other. We have already touched upon the preparation and work of the professional teacher. The first essential for the minister is that he should be a master of those biblical and theological studies in respect of which the teachers ought to be able to look to him for inspiration and guidance. But he also needs sufficient knowledge of educational theory and practice to enable him to enter into the teacher's work with understanding and appreciation, and thus to make the presentation of his own material relevant to the teacher's use of it. As a preacher the minister himself teaches, and he should learn from his theological college how to make preaching educative as well as prophetic. He is likely in most cases to be drawn into the direct work of teaching, whether in Sunday school, young people's societies or adult groups, within the church or in church day schools; in some countries he will certainly be called upon to give religious instruction in day schools under the system approved by the state. He should therefore be given whatever help, with regard to educational method, it may be possible to provide as part of his course of ministerial training. He will thereafter be the more likely to seize as he should the opportunities afforded by special short courses on the principles and practice of teaching, and to value aright those personal relationships with teachers in his own area which must inevitably be mutually profitable.

Worship introduces a fundamental distinction between the life of the Christian society and that of every secular group. It is the adoration of the eternal God who dwells beyond the limitations of our thought and knowledge. At the same time, if the world is to be known as a sphere of the divine activity, we need a more determined effort to use the daily texture of experience within the church, community and state to supply the content of Christian acts of

praise, thanksgiving, penitence and petition. The training
of ministers and teachers in the use of educational method
in the conduct of worship has already been mentioned.
While corporate worship is itself a training of the mind and
spirit there is room for definite guidance in habits of private
prayer and meditation and for the encouragement of prayer
by groups of people who have professional or other interests in common.

(d) *The Church in Relation to Public Education where
the Government is Responsive to Christian Opinion.*
The church is confronted in the world today with a variety of state policies in regard to religious education. Very
generally a widespread system of church schools has been
superseded by the provision of public or state schools for
all classes of the population. The church moreover has
found it difficult, owing to her limited financial resources,
to maintain her schools on a level of efficiency comparable
with that of the better equipped and more adequately
staffed state schools. The choice here does not lie between
struggling to preserve a number of unsatisfactory schools
and closing them all. We believe that it is an essential part
of the church's witness that at such a time she concentrate
her efforts upon creating and maintaining a smaller number of schools of differing types which by their distinctive
quality serve as a demonstration of educational standards
that are fully Christian. This is shown by the achievements
of many denominational schools in countries of religiously
mixed populations.

Since the mass of her members always moves slowly toward a new and more sensitive Christian conscience in matters of social obligation, it would seem that the church must
today, as in past centuries, encourage and protect minority
groups of Christians who protest against contemporary
society, are critical of the organized churches and desire

to experiment in education with what they consider a more Christian way of life. Her history makes plain the debt which subsequent generations owe to rebels and explorers, and, while they will never be the main body of her people, she ought to be at pains to retain them in her spiritual household and to safeguard them in what may seem their eccentric and unconventional ways.

In some lands provision for Christian teaching finds a place in the schools maintained by the state. This plan makes possible, as perhaps no other could, the diffusion of knowledge of the contents of the Bible and of Christian belief throughout the population. It is, however, important not to overestimate the importance of the inclusion of religious teaching in the curriculum of a school. Its effect may even be harmful if the teacher lacks conviction or adequate training. If the majority of the population are in general sympathy with Christian standards and values, church and state should find no difficulty in working together to assure a religious education to those who desire it. Obviously, freedom of conscience must be respected and no coercion exerted on those who do not wish religious training for themselves or their children. But the Christian or other religious elements in the population should not be deprived of their right to receive a completely religious education. Freedom of conscience in education has been too negatively conceived. There are both a liberty not to have religious training forced where it is objected to, and a liberty to have it provided where consciences feel it essential for the education of citizens of the state and of the kingdom of God. If there are incompatible religious groups to be considered, two or more types of religious education may have to be provided.

Here is one of the situations where Christians must seek for the largest possible agreement in what they ask or the

civil authorities will content themselves with supplying a
secular education to avoid possible sectarian strife. Since
the beginning of the present century, a great advance has
been made in at least one country where previously suspicions and conflicts arising from disagreement between the
churches as to the content of Christian teaching in state
schools had gravely hindered the progress of both general
and specifically religious education. A large part of this
mischief was due to laying emphasis upon what must not be
taught because it would be sectarian. When attention was
drawn to the inadequacy of the syllabuses of biblical instruction that were in use, education authorities invited
the cooperation of the churches and the teachers in drawing
up agreed syllabuses satisfactory from both the religious
and the educational points of view. A resulting emphasis
upon what all parties would wish included has greatly enriched the content of the teaching, has created a far more
Christian atmosphere of mutual trust, and has led to active
cooperation in securing facilities for teachers to equip themselves more fully for their task. Governments and local
authorities which do not take the initiative in such a movement may yet respond to it if churches and teachers make
common cause in promoting it. In some cases the syllabus
agreed upon in this way for use in state schools is used also
for certain days in the week in the church schools, and the
special teaching characteristic of the denomination is given
on the remaining days.

There is another plan which obtains in some countries
where church and state are legally separate. By this the
churches, with the approval of a majority in the community,
have arranged with the educational authority that schools
should release at stated hours, for Christian instruction,
pupils whose parents desire it, and have come to an agreement among themselves as to the courses offered and the

conduct of such instruction. This plan has the advantage of leaving the church at liberty to direct the specifically religious education given.

It may fairly be asked of the state that if it permits religious instruction to be given in its schools it should insure as far as possible that such instruction be treated as seriously as that in other subjects and as of equal importance. Unfortunately this is often not the case. Teachers should be given as good opportunities of learning how to give religious instruction as they have of acquiring competence in the teaching of subjects commonly called secular, whether they receive their training in colleges specially provided for prospective kindergarten and primary teachers or in the education departments of universities. When they have completed their training and are at work in the schools, teachers should be encouraged to avail themselves of further help such as university extra-mural departments or properly qualified voluntary organizations provide in co-operation with education authorities for the study of the Bible and methods of teaching it. As in other subjects, specialist teachers should be appointed, when the size of the school justifies it, and particularly in secondary schools, to give some of the more advanced teaching and to assist and guide other teachers who share in the work of religious instruction. It is of course most desirable that such specialist teachers should be also qualified for the teaching of some subject or subjects other than religious knowledge and should not run the risk of appearing to be interested only in religion as something apart from all other aspects of education and life.

Colleges and universities which are precluded by the basis on which they are founded from maintaining a divinity faculty or providing courses in the study of religion as well as from holding services of public worship for their

members, may well give full facilities to recognized inter-
denominational movements, such as the Student Christian
Movement and the Y.M.C.A. or Y.W.C.A., for carrying
on those forms of religious education and fellowship which
so patently meet the needs of students and link the colleges
and universities with the church. Furthermore, while it is
obviously essential that distinction in intellectual capacity
and achievement should be required of those who teach or
direct undergraduate and graduate students, and while in
state institutions religious tests are inadmissible, full regard
should be paid in making college and university appoint-
ments to the moral and spiritual qualities of men and
women who will inevitably influence so deeply the future
leaders in the life of the community.

In schools supported by public funds or on Christian
foundations, the church cannot feel it to be good that any
pupils who will profit by the education supplied should be
excluded on grounds of race or social status.

(e) *Christian Education in a Non-Christian Environment.* The greatest opportunity of the church in relation
to public education lies in those countries where there is no
developed system of state schools but where a friendly government welcomes the pioneering efforts of Christian missions in the provision of schools. Here religion is regarded
as essential to the reintegration of a community which has
lost the social, economic and spiritual cohesion it possessed
under primitive tribal conditions. Thus generous grants
from public funds are frequently made to the support of
Christian schools. Christian teachers are given exceptional
freedom both to express their deepest convictions and to
experiment in new methods. The situation has its own
dangers. Chief of these is the danger that, under the pressure of an extending system of schools and rising standards
of efficiency, the distinctive Christian witness in education

may be lost. The remedy lies in maintaining the supply of teachers of ability and conviction and in continuous vigilance in the selection of objectives in educational policy.

Even where the state or the community are not Christian there is often a friendly attitude toward Christian work. Where the church has in some cases succeeded in creating a satisfactory system of education in her own name, she has every right to claim freedom to continue such work. She will use to the full this opportunity for training Christian leadership. At the same time, as she requires for her own members liberty of conscience in non-Christian communities, so she will respect a like liberty when non-Christians come within her institutions. In such schools the church must not oppose the claim of the nation to ask for all its members a proper loyalty toward the state. She herself teaches that we have special responsibilities and affections toward the country in which we live. She has an urgent task in her own schools in developing the synthesis of the appreciation of all that is good in the culture of each nation and race with the overruling loyalty to God who is Father of all the nations. She must beware of a syncretism which loses the distinctive significance of her message, while at the same time she must welcome everything in the background of each nation which is close to the mind of Christ.

Already in many countries the state, learning perhaps from the example of the church which has pioneered the way, and using its larger powers and resources, is often providing education of a higher standard than is provided in Christian schools. Where this is the case, the church must regard excellence as in accordance with the mind of God. She must not accept a tinge of added piety as an excuse for inefficiency. She will not lightly relinquish the advantages in the training of Christian leadership in her own schools. She must, however, see that the education which she offers is of the best. Where she cannot achieve this she must beware of identifying the name of Christ in the eyes of men with the relatively inefficient. By the concentration of her own resources, she may then in some schools and universities both maintain a high level of scholarship and pioneer in her special field of Christian thought and worship.

In countries where the state is undertaking the work of general education, and where it can give no official permission for Christian teaching in state universities and schools, the church may well claim that, on purely academic grounds, no education is complete which arbitrarily excludes one whole field of human experience and history. She will recognize that a state in which Christians are a minority cannot enforce Christian teaching, but she will point out that the education offered would be inadequate, unless those who desired to study the Bible and its message and its place in human history had some opportunity to do so.

The church may further exercise her influence through the teachers in state schools. These may be her members, or may be won into her membership. Even if there is no place for formal religious instruction, there will be abundant opportunity for Christian work both through personal influence and in the manner of presentation of nonreligious subjects. The Christian teacher will not unfairly force his religious position, but equally he need not hide it. Finally there are the openings for voluntary religious work among students to which we have referred in a previous paragraph.

In many countries the situation is far less favorable. In some the state, while allowing considerable liberty for Christian work, yet requires of all members of the nation acts of homage in various forms, which may involve a turning aside of that worship which may be given to God alone. This claim of the state is accentuated where for temporary political reasons the state is anxious to build up an intensive loyalty to itself. Only general principles can here be suggested. The church will acknowledge that there is a proper patriotism in subordination to the God of all nations. Sometimes the rising tide of national loyalty may seem to blind men to the claims of other nations. But there is a proper sense of citizenship, and where this is lacking the state has the right to promote a greater loyalty to the nation. The church will remember that the charge to render to Caesar the things that are Caesar's was first given concerning a non-Christian power.

The state today frequently insists on retaining all education in its own hands. This policy we regard as unfortunate in that it prevents an enriching variety in educational work. Even where such state education is Christian, a dominant confession may sometimes threaten the freedom of religious minorities. Elsewhere the state is using education as an instrument of propaganda for inculcating views of life which negate the Christian faith. In all cases we should claim for the church and for all Christian parents the right to instruct their children in what they believe to be the truth. The church is at one with all true scholarship in every sphere in insisting that education may not submit to the bias of propaganda but must preserve the pure and disinterested pursuit of truth.

In those countries where the present political situation is accentuating difficulties, the church will do all she can to preserve the favor of the state. In the last resort, however, she must maintain for her members their liberty of conscience and preserve them from idolatry. The early church learned to render to Caesar his due, yet suffered martyrdom rather than render to Caesar the worship due to

God. The Christian may and should give a respect to past or present political leaders, but he must withhold worship. The point where patriotic reverence becomes idolatry is not easy to define. It is the point where an absolute loyalty is given to an external human authority rather than to the voice of God made known in Christ and in the inward voice of conscience and truth. If and where this point is reached, Christian teachers and students must and will still be ready to suffer persecution.

When all other openings are forbidden, the church must do what she can through parents and through such ministry of Christian teachers in homes as she can provide. It is a grievous circumscription of her work but it may have to be accepted for the present time of hostility to religion. Such periods have not in the past been long, and the church may hearten herself by recalling her history. Where she is allowed to retain her institutions of learning, these should be conserved even if opportunities for Christian influence are restricted. She must think not in decades but in generations. The situation may change, will surely change some day, and it is folly to sacrifice strategic centers of Christian education. These are times for following a New Testament precedent — to throw out anchors and wish for the day.

The church's largest contribution to education, like her supreme ministry to human life, is her gospel, with its interpretation of existence and its inspiration to live worthily. Where life is without meaning, education becomes futile. Where it is ignobly conceived, education is debased. Where it is viewed in the light of God's purpose in Christ, it assumes divine significance. It is not the methods by which her gospel is taught which are of first importance. They will differ according to the educational system preferred by various nations and by various communions in the church. It is all-important that her gospel should supply the presuppositions of all education, by whatever agency it is given, and create the spiritual atmosphere which pervades every institution of true learning. " In thy Light shall we see light."

SALIENT POINTS

(1) The church is concerned that every child and adult shall receive the fullest education consistent with his capacities and that no discrimination in educational opportunity be made on the basis of race or social status. But she must make plain that no education is adequate without the living encounter with God and the response of personal faith.

(2) For any education worthy of the name truth is supreme, and there must be freedom to seek and to teach it. In some lands governments attempt to control all the agencies which influence belief and behavior. They abridge the church's right to educate her children in the Christian faith. She must protest against a state monopoly of education and claim liberty to carry on her work through such means as youth organizations and institutions for training Christian leadership.

(3) It is the church's aim to educate free persons under law to Christ. Freedom, in her view, is not a natural gift. The freedom which she seeks is both liberty from the deceit of evil passions within the heart, and the strength of character to preserve liberty of conscience under external pressure. It is her conviction that personality attains this freedom and completeness only in obedience to God.

(4) While opposed to any deification of the community or the state, Christians must sympathize with the effort to restore unity in a time of social disintegration and must recognize education as a powerful means toward this end.

The church is opposed to any education which stimulates unbridled individualism and must affirm the basis for social solidarity which God has given in the relationships of the family and the community.

(5) A characteristic feature of our time is the response made by youth to the appeal of political leaders who offer them a part in the building of the nation. This gives a sense of community, definiteness of purpose and demand upon their whole energies. The complete fulfillment of their desires will be found only when Christ is proclaimed as Lord and when the church offers them real community in devotion to his purpose for mankind.

(6) There are today both in the older and younger churches an immense opening and an immense responsibility for Christian education. Many more Christian teachers are needed; for the spirit of Christ can be conveyed only through persons to persons.

(7) The church must educate those of her members who are parents, schoolteachers, professors in institutions of higher learning, Sunday school workers and leaders in youth organizations and in adult education. These all share in her ministry of teaching. She must see to it that her clergy are thoroughly equipped with biblical and other theological learning and with such knowledge and skill as shall make them competent teachers and partners of other teachers in the work of education.

(8) In considering her task we discover that frequently an impediment more serious than any restriction from without is the disunion of the church's own forces. Where educational leaders in community and state are eager to cooperate with her, they are perplexed by the differing proposals of her various communions and embarrassed by the rivalries between them. They hesitate to involve public institutions in sectarian strife. The lack of a common

mind on the fundamentals of Christian faith and life has thus pushed many states into secularist systems of education. If the church is to discharge her teaching duty, she must bring her communions into a common front on educational issues and unite her forces in fulfilling this urgent task.

V. REPORT OF THE SECTION ON THE UNIVERSAL CHURCH AND THE WORLD OF NATIONS *

1. THE PRESENT SITUATION

AT A TIME when the hearts of men fail them for fear, the conference calls upon the members of the churches to remain steadfast in their faith in God and in Jesus Christ the Saviour of all mankind.

The years that have passed since the close of the World War have witnessed a great change in the public temper in every land. Problems which the war created, left unsolved, or aggravated, have resulted in a state of tension which has now found expression in a resurgent nationalism, in selfish isolation or in antagonistic national groupings, in rearmament on a colossal scale, and in the universal fear that a war which all nations dread is at hand. At the same time the economic depression has increased within every nation the conviction that it must rely upon itself for its own security with little regard for considerations of international morality. Where even ten years ago there was in a great part of the world a spirit of optimistic faith in the creation of a true international order, there are now bewilderment and dejection. In such a world the duty of the church is to

* The report, after receiving the approval of the section, was submitted to the conference substantially in its present form. The conference received the report, referred it back to the section for revision in the light of the discussion and commended it to the serious and favorable consideration of the churches. The report was revised by the section and approved by it in its present form.

call all men to repentance, to faith and to a compassionate concern for the multitudes who suffer. We need not despair: the world belongs to God; to believe in his power and love is not to escape from reality but to stand upon the rock of the only certainty that is offered to men. The church calls therefore to the world of men, of which it is itself a part, not only to rise to a new level of effort and self-devotion, but to believe in the God and Father of our Lord Jesus Christ, who has overcome the world.

2. THE ECUMENICAL CHURCH

A special ground of faith and courage amid the perplexities of our age is that the Christian church is becoming truly ecumenical. The missionary movement of the past century carried forward the sense of world mission inherent in the biblical records, making the bounds of the Christian community coextensive with the habitable globe. This movement has been the principal sign that the church was alive to the God-given vision of the church universal. Moreover the churches are realizing anew that the church is one. We say this in full recognition of the fact that between many of the churches which we represent there is a lack of true fellowship, and that the church of Rome is not represented in our midst. At the same time, the emergence in different parts of the world of political systems usurping the role of churches and demanding the absolute allegiance of men and women is awakening in Christians in every land a deepened loyalty to Christ and the church and a fresh sense of their need of solidarity in Christ.

It is important to bear in mind in this connection the fundamental distinction between " ecumenical " and " international." The term " international " necessarily accepts the division of mankind into separate nations as a natural if not a final state of affairs. The term " ecumenical " refers to the expression within history of the given unity of the church. The one starts from the fact of division and the other from the fact of unity in Christ. The thought and action of the church are international in so far as the church must operate in a world in which the historical Christian bodies share with the rest of mankind the division into national and racial groups. They are ecumenical in so far as they attempt to realize the *una sancta,* the fellowship of Christians who acknowledge the one Lord.

This fact of the ecumenical character of the church carries with it the important consequence that the church brings to the task of achieving a better international order an insight which is not to be derived from ordinary political sources. To those who are struggling to realize human brotherhood in a world where disruptive nationalism and aggressive imperialism make such brotherhood seem unreal, the church offers not an ideal but a fact, man united not by his aspiration but by the love of God.

True ecumenicity therefore must be the goal of all our efforts. Churches must be not simply tolerant one toward another but concerned about unity one with the other. Very especially at a time when in parts of the world " some members of the body suffer " and others are still weak, must the privileged and stronger members remember the words, " Bear ye one another's burdens and so fulfill the law of Christ."

Moreover, lack of unity conflicts seriously with the ultimate and supreme purposes of the church. These purposes are and must remain to proclaim the gospel of God's love in Jesus Christ to all mankind, to administer the sacraments, to fulfill the Christian ideal of fellowship and to guide the souls of her children in the ways of holiness. No other activity in which she may engage can be a substitute for these. For the church is supremely concerned with persons, and world problems have their roots ultimately in the hearts of persons who " must be born again." She must speak therefore in the name of God to the individual men and women who make up the nations and must announce to them, in language they can understand, the news of the world's Saviour. As the greatest need of the world is new men, and the church's chief opponents in our time aspire to change the very structure of human nature in those whom they control, the church of Christ throughout the world should work unceasingly for human renewal and the cure of souls in his name and through his strength " who maketh all things new."

At the same time the church has a concern with civilization in general. With penitence, on the one hand, because of the share of responsibility belonging to many of her members for the present state of the world, with thanksgiving, on the other, because she has been herself under God the source of some of the chief treasures that the world possesses, the church must recognize her concern with the secular order. With her members active in every sphere of life, resident in every land, owing allegiance to every form of state, the church is concerned with the whole world and the whole of life within it. The Christian church, acknowledging Christ's work of redemption, possesses a unique insight into the problems of human relationship. Knowing man and " what is in man " Christians will not be elated with an unchristian hope; knowing Christ and what is " in Christ " they will not be cast down with an unchristian despair. There comes a call to the church to face in the light of Christ all the facts that may be gathered from every quarter, and thereafter, in the spirit and through the grace of Christ, to work for the manifestation of the new divine order which appeared in the cross and resurrection of the Son of God.

3. THE KINGDOM OF GOD AND THE INTERNATIONAL ORDER

Before entering upon the discussion of any of the concrete difficulties which face Christians in regard to the international order, it is necessary to recall the dual aspect of the Christian attitude toward this and all kindred problems.

No international order which can be devised by human effort may be equated with the kingdom of God. Much of the disillusionment about international affairs to be found among Christians is due to the fact that the hopes vested in specific schemes for international betterment were of an almost religious quality, and it was forgotten that to all human institutions clings the taint of sin.

On the other hand, it is erroneous to hold that our hope in the kingdom of God has no bearing upon the practical choices that men must make within the present order. The attitude of Christians toward specific proposals in the political sphere should be governed by their obedience to the living God and their understanding of his purpose in Christ.

A true conception of international order requires a recognition of the fact that the state, whether it admits it or not, is not autonomous but is under the ultimate governance of God. This relates not only to its dealings with its own citizens but to its dealings with other states and the individuals within them. While therefore we recognize fully the need for continuous adjustment of international arrangements, we assert that the demand for constancy and fidelity may be made upon states as well as upon individuals. While the trustee responsibility of states differentiates their duty from that of individuals, it remains true that righteousness exalteth a nation and that nations, like individuals, are under the judgment of God.

4. INHERENT DIFFICULTIES IN THE ESTABLISHMENT OF INTERNATIONAL ORDER

We must recognize that relations between states have not been brought under the rule of law in the same way as relations between citizens or social groups within the borders of states. The life of the state — or at least of civilized or constitutional states — represents a union between law and force. Thus is insured the working of two processes, separable in theory but inextricably blended in practice — the observance and enforcement of the law and the constant and steady development of the law to conform to changing social needs.

When we turn to the field of interstate relations we find a very different condition. Here law and force have never yet been brought into an effective working partnership. The various political units into which the world is divided stand side by side without any organic connection. They are not merely separate states but separate societies differing in custom and tradition, in outlook and culture, which are among the principal elements that go to the making of law and provide law with so much of its authority. International law, which is the body of rules laid down in treaties and other documents for the conduct of states, is incomplete, and has not commanded general respect because it originates in a sphere remote from ordinary men and women and has not yet been brought into effective touch with their social consciousness. Relations between states have been and still are conceived and carried on chiefly in terms of power. The traditional criterion of what constitutes a " great power " is a standing challenge to Christian people, more especially to those who are citizens of " great powers."

Various means have been suggested on the political plane for dealing with this problem. The simplest and most radical is to abolish the system of power-relations by subordinating the concept of independent sovereignty through the establishment of a federal system. Another solution, attempted in the League of Nations, is to create an organization providing for constant and regular cooperation between states, thus promoting common habits and standards which may in time form the basis of a common law.

So far as the present evil is political, the heart of it is to be found in the claim of each national state to be judge in its own cause. The abandonment of that claim, and the abrogation of absolute national sovereignty at least to that extent, is a duty that the church should urge upon the nations.

But political remedies of this kind are not enough. The evil lies deeper down, in the ingrained habits and attitudes which find expression in the power-relationship. Within the state, power has been curbed by constitutional checks and has been made subject to a sense of responsibility. In the international field and often in relationship to colonial dependencies power is still, broadly speaking, irresponsible. It is here that the Christian church and individual Christians have an opportunity to bring their influence to bear upon international relations. For the power-relationship is not merely uncivilized: it is also utterly unchristian. " Render unto Caesar " is not a counsel of acquiescence or of despair. Unless we are prepared to cut our life into two utterly separate halves, we must admit that it is our duty to do all that in us lies to bring Caesar — the traditions and practices of government — to the recognition of his duty to God.

All law, international as well as national, must be based on a common ethos, that is, a common foundation of moral convictions. To the creation of such a common foundation in moral conviction the church, as a supra-national society with a profound sense of the historical realities and of the worth of human personality, has a great contribution to make.

5. THE CONDITIONS OF PEACEFUL CHANGE

The fact that no superior political agency exists to impose from time to time a new order in international affairs to conform to changing needs means not that the existing order will remain static but that change can occur in only one of two ways: by voluntary action, or by force or the menace of force.

It therefore particularly devolves upon Christians to devote themselves to securing by voluntary action of their nations such changes in the international order as are from time to time required to avoid injustice and to promote equality of opportunity for individuals throughout the world. Christian influence to this end cannot be made effective without adequate factual knowledge. To meet this initial need Christians should take measures to obtain information on world conditions more adequate and reliable than that now furnished by the secular and nationalistic agencies, which are too prone to ignore or belittle the needs of alien peoples or to express those needs in terms of sacrifice to be made by nations other than their own.

Once the need of change is apprehended its accomplishment depends upon governmental action. This will require of statesmen and politicians a broader vision than now exists of the true welfare of their nation. The heads of states, under whatever form of government, are ultimately dependent upon the support of their people who must make it clear that they are prepared to accept temporary sacrifices in order that a greater good may ultimately emerge.

The unequal distribution of natural bounties is one of the causes of war, if control is used to create a monopoly of national advantages. Christian people should move their governments to abstain from such policies and to provide a reasonable equality of economic opportunity.

If, however, primary responsibility rests upon those of the Christian peoples for whom change means sharing with others, some responsibility devolves also upon Christians in less fortunate lands. Many voices in all nations are lifted in these days in favor of a more just international order and the removal of inequalities of opportunity. The achievement of the practical results can only be retarded if through the overeagerness of some the impression is created that equality of opportunity is sought not as an end in itself but as a means of reversing in their favor inequalities such as now exist.

6. ATTEMPTS TO ORGANIZE AN INTERNATIONAL ORDER

(a) *The League of Nations.* Among the many organizations interested in the achievement of international order the most notable is the League of Nations. While it is necessary to recognize that the league has not been able to fulfill the hopes which have been reposed in it and that decided changes must take place if the league is to be brought into greater harmony with international needs and with its own ideal, it is important that Christian peoples should have a clear conception of its status and character.

The league is not a government; it cannot take decisions except in so far as the constituent governments concur.

Those who criticize the league for what it has done or failed to do are really criticizing the governments of the member states or certain particular governments. The tendency to endow the league with qualities which it does not or cannot possess, and therefore to indulge in excessive expectations, has been responsible for much disillusionment and confusion of mind.

The league is not a church. Its concern is with the world of day to day politics and administration. The fact that through the league states have pledged themselves to a great ideal, that of peace and peaceful cooperation, should not lead Christians to identify their hopes with present-day realities. However, as a standing agency of cooperation between fifty or more independent governments the league represents the most considerable effort yet made in the world's history to enable the governments to consult together, to plan together and to act together. It is an attempt to establish a system of political interdependence corresponding with the economic interdependence characteristic of modern civilization.

The assertion is frequently made that the league has failed. Admittedly the covenant has not been fully observed and vindicated by the states who signed it. The facts of the last six years speak for themselves. But the idea on which the league was founded — that of international cooperation — has not been disproved. No alternative conception or method of comparable range has come to light in the intervening period, and the need for an agency of international cooperation is as great as ever, if not greater. Moreover, where in the political field obstacles arising out of the system of power politics have not been maintained to the extreme point, and where, as in the technical work of the league and the international labor organization, such obstacles intervene to only a slight extent, much success has been achieved. This only emphasizes the fact that the real issue that confronts us both at Geneva and elsewhere is that of power politics and the attitude of mind which it represents. That is the root problem of all international politics. Until it is solved the world community so often lightly spoken of as a fact must remain an aspiration.

The league therefore is a means to certain ends. In proportion as these ends are desirable so will their attainment make a large demand on those qualities of energy, good faith and readiness to pay the price which as we have already stated are the conditions of effective international action.

(b) *Permanent Court of International Justice.* Important also as an instrument for the peaceful settlement of justiciable disputes is the Permanent Court of International Justice at The Hague. The existence of such a tribunal deprives nations of any excuse for having recourse to force for the settlement of such disputes as involve the interpretation and application of admitted international obligations.

(c) *Treaties.* International order not only comes into being through world-wide organizations such as those above mentioned, but also by arbitration treaties and such other agreements as are not exclusive nor based on antagonism to other nations.

(d) *The Church as Peacemaker.* Nevertheless, while giving discriminating support to work for peace and justice both political and social through the League of Nations and kindred organizations, the church cannot leave the duty of peacemaking to political agencies. The church is itself called to a ministry of reconciliation in a world riven by fears, suspicions and grievances. The church should be able by the leading of the Spirit to discover characteristically Christian ways of intervening as a healing and reconciling influence in a world of conflict.

7. THE CHURCH AND WAR

We approach this part of our subject with a profound sense of its urgency and of the inadequacy of the best that we can say. We know that multitudes are oppressed by the actual menace of war. While we may seek to influence actions which may avert the immediate danger, our main task is to probe the underlying sources of the evil and point to the ultimate remedy.

Here again our starting point is the universal fellowship of Christians, the *una sancta*. All Christians acknowledge one Lord, whose claim upon them is such as to transcend all other loyalties. Here is the first obligation of the church, to be in living fact the church, a society with a unity so deep as to be indestructible by earthly divisions of race or nation or class.

Wars, the occasions of war, and all situations which conceal the fact of conflict under the guise of outward peace, are marks of a world to which the church is charged to proclaim the gospel of redemption. War involves compulsory enmity, diabolical outrage against human personality, and a wanton distortion of the truth. War is a particular demonstration of the power of sin in this world and a defiance of the righteousness of God as revealed in Jesus Christ and him crucified. No justification of war must be allowed to conceal or minimize this fact.

In all situations the Christian has to bear in mind both the absolute command, " Thou shalt love thy neighbor as thyself," and the obligation to do what most nearly corresponds to that command in the circumstances confronting him. His action may be but a poor expression of perfect love; the man is caught in a sinful situation, to the evil of which he may have contributed much or little. The best that is possible falls far " short of the glory of God " and is, in that sense, sinful; each man must bear his share of the corporate sin which has rendered impossible any better course; and we all have to confess that "our righteousnesses are as filthy rags." Yet to do what appears as relatively best is an absolute duty before God, and to fail in this is to incur positive guilt.

The search for the will of God is a matter of agonizing perplexity for the Christian whose country is involved in war. We have to recognize two widely divergent views regarding war, along with several that are intermediate. One view hopes for the elimination of war by the power of God working in history through the religious and moral enlightenment of men and the exercise of their free wills; the other view regards man as so bound in the necessities of a sinful world that war will be eliminated only as a consequence of the return of Christ in glory.

In practice this divergence issues in three main positions which are sincerely and conscientiously held by Christians:

(1) Some believe that war, especially in its modern form, is always sin, being a denial of the nature of God as love, of the redemptive way of the cross, and of the community of the Holy Spirit; that war is always ultimately destructive in its effects, and ends in futility by corrupting even the noblest purpose for which it is waged; and that the church will become a creative, regenerative and reconciling instrument for the healing of the nations only as it renounces war absolutely. They are therefore constrained to refuse to take part in war themselves, to plead among their fellows for a similar repudiation of war in favor of a better way, and to replace military force by methods of active peacemaking.

(2) Some would participate only in "just wars." Here there are at least two points of view, depending upon the definition of the "just war." The first view holds that

Christians should participate only in such wars as are justifiable on the basis of international law. They believe that in a sinful world the state has the duty, under God, to use force when law and order are threatened. Wars against transgressors of international agreements and pacts are comparable with police measures and Christians are obliged to participate in them. But if the state requires its citizens to participate in wars which cannot be thus justified, they believe that Christians should refuse, for the state has no right to force its citizens to take part in sinful actions. Many would add that no war should be regarded as " just " if the government concerned fails to submit the subject of dispute or *casus belli* to arbitration, conciliation or judgment of an international authority.

Those who hold the second view would regard a " just war " as one waged to vindicate what they believe to be an essential Christian principle: to defend the victims of wanton aggression or to secure freedom for the oppressed. They would urge that it was a Christian duty, where all other means had failed, to take up arms. In so doing they would look to the verdict of conscience as their ultimate sanction. While recognizing the general importance of supporting civil or international order, the maintenance of such order in the present imperfect state of society cannot be a final obligation. The Christian, though he must be willing to accept martyrdom for himself, cannot expose others to it by refusing to fight for them.

(3) Some, while also stressing the Christian obligation to work for peace and mutual understanding among the nations, hold nevertheless that no such effort can end war in this world. Moreover, while recognizing that political authority is frequently administered in a selfish and immoral way, they nevertheless believe that the state is the

agent divinely appointed to preserve a nation from the detrimental effects of anarchic and criminal tendencies among its members, and to maintain its existence against the aggression of its neighbors.   It is therefore a Christian's duty to obey the political authority as far as possible and to refrain from everything that is apt to weaken it. This means that normally a Christian must take up arms for his country.   Only when he is absolutely certain that his country is fighting for a wrong cause — for example, in case of unjustifiable war of aggression — has the ordinary citizen a right to refuse military service.

Of those who hold this view, some would admit that individuals may be called directly by God to refuse categorically to take part in any war and so draw attention to the perverted nature of a world in which wars are possible.   In either case the individual must recognize in principle the significance of the state and be willing to accept punishment by the authorities for violating the national law.

We do not affirm that any one of these positions can be held to represent the only possible Christian attitude.   The church must insist that the perplexity itself is a sign of the sin in which its members are implicated.   It cannot rest in permanent acquiescence in the continuance of these differences but should do all that is possible to promote the study of the problem by people of different views meeting together to learn from one another as they seek to understand the purpose of God as revealed in Jesus Christ.   Recognizing that its members are also called to live within the secular state or nation and that in the event of war a conflict of duties is inevitable, it should help them discover God's will, should honor their conscientious decisions, whether they are led to participate in or to abstain from war, and maintain with both alike the full fellowship of the body of

Christ. It should call them to repent and to seek together that deliverance from the entangling evil which can be found in Christ alone.

The church must call its members to confess their share in the common guilt of mankind for the continuance of war and the spirit of war among the nations. Notwithstanding the notable efforts for peace which have been made within the church, clergy and laity alike have not done what they ought to have done to remove the causes of war by raising their voices against attitudes and policies making for war, and have not proclaimed with boldness the word of truth in time of war. Moreover they have often been guilty of greed, selfishness, distrust, and pride of race and nation, thus contributing to the embittering of relations among the nations. At the same time, the church must call its members to give " diligence to keep the unity of the Spirit in the bond of peace." Church members should earnestly strive to remove in their own lives every attitude and practice deriving from political, social and racial differences which are the seeds of war, and should seek the fruit of the Spirit, " love, joy, peace, long-suffering kindness, goodness, faithfulness, meekness, self-control."

The church should remind its members that the principle of the unconditional supremacy of the state or nation advanced either in time of peace or of war, is incompatible with the church's faith in Jesus Christ as its only Lord and is therefore unacceptable as the final norm of judgment or action. It is the church's duty to serve the nation in which it is placed, but the greatest service which it can render is to remain steadfast and loyal to its Lord and to test rigorously all claims of national interest by his gospel.

The church, confessing its faith in redemption through Jesus Christ, sees in every man a " brother for whom Christ died." In time of war, as in time of peace, it should pray not only for the nation in which God has placed it, but also for the enemies of that nation. If Christians in warring nations pray according to the pattern of prayer given by their Lord, they will not be " praying against " one another. The church should witness in word, in sacramental life and in action to the reality of the kingdom of God which transcends the world of nations. It should proclaim and obey the commandment of the Lord, " Love your enemies."

8. THE CHURCH'S WITNESS

The contemporary situation in its pathos and complexity presents an unprecedented challenge to the Church of Christ Universal. In what way shall the church, in loyalty to her Lord and her essential nature and with full cognizance of and concern for the world, address herself to the existing conditions inside and outside the Christian community?

It is essential to remember, if anything effective is to be achieved, that Christians should be fully aware of their great responsibility to the world, but anxious at the same time to discharge this responsibility in a distinctively Christian manner. The church herself is the leaven by which Christ transforms the life of society and nations. There can be no true Christian action which is not rooted in full participation in the worship of the church and animated by zeal for the expression of true community in things both spiritual and material.

With these things in view we submit the following considerations which have a practical bearing upon the witness of the church.

(a) *Removal of Racial Barriers.* The church dishonors its claim to ecumenical reality if it allows, even under the pressure of situations of great and genuine difficulty, the presence of racial barriers within it. We call attention here both to the acceptance of the color bar in certain churches and to the more widely diffused and less acknowledged evil of anti-Semitism, whereby not only have terrible sufferings been imposed upon the Jews by states historically Christian, but membership within the church denied or made difficult to those of the race to which our Lord belonged after the flesh.

(b) *Religious Freedom.* An essential element in a better international order is freedom of religion. This is an implication of the faith of the church. Moreover, the ecumenical character of the church compels it to view the question of religious freedom as an international problem: all parts of the church are concerned that religious freedom be everywhere secured. We are, therefore, deeply concerned with the limitations that are increasingly being imposed in the modern world. We affirm the primary right to religious worship and the converse right to refuse compliance with any form of worship unacceptable on grounds of conscience. We affirm the right to public witness to religion and the right to religious teaching especially in the nurture of the young. In pleading for such rights we do not ask for any privilege to be granted to Christians that is denied to others. While the liberty with which Christ has set us free can neither be given nor destroyed by any government, Christians, because of that inner freedom, are both jealous for its outward expression and solicitous that all men should have freedom in religious life. The rights which Christian discipleship demands are such as are good for all men, and no nation has ever suffered by reason of granting such liberties.

While affirming these principles we deprecate any attempt by Christians to secure under the shelter of the power or prestige of their nations any privileges in other countries in such matters as civil status, the holding of property or language of education.   This does not invalidate the rights of Christians in their own countries to make such claims as they are entitled to make in common with other nationals.

At the same time we call upon the churches we represent to guard against the sin of themselves conniving at repression of churches and religious bodies of a faith and order differing from their own.   The ideal of ecumenicity demands that the church in its various branches set an example to the world of toleration for all, and specifically for members of minority Christian communions.   The occasion to further the cause of international understanding lies immediately to hand and is within the power of the churches to use forthwith, namely, "to do good to all men and especially toward them that are of the household of faith."

(c) *Mutual Church Aid*. Ecumenical solidarity implies that the churches which are strong in resources should be ready to render help to those which are weak or in distress anywhere throughout the world.   But in every instance the required assistance, whether money, counsel or leadership, should be given without an accompanying claim to the right to dominate.   Particularly the younger churches, which are the fruit of the church's missionary effort, have special claim upon the concern of the Christian church.

(d) *Ecumenical Education*.   The church is by nature ecumenical, but few of its members have as yet come to realize the full implication of this fact.   In order to give content to this Christian affirmation we must attempt to educate church members in the understanding of the actual witness, life and problems of other churches than their own.   Theological faculties and seminaries have a particularly important task in this connection.   They should introduce into their program the study of the contemporary theology — dogmatic as well as practical — of all branches

of the Christian church and enable their students to enter
into personal contact with the church life of other confes-
sions and in other countries. The future of the ecumenical
movement depends largely on whether a generation of
Christians can be formed, who, while rooted in their own
traditions, are willing by much patience, scrupulous fair-
ness and also by critical insight and complete frankness to
labor for a deeper understanding between the churches.

(e) *Education for Peace.* The churches should employ
the agencies of Christian education, alike in the nurture of
children and in the guidance of adult members, to " follow after the things which make for peace." This should
include a study of world problems and contemporary
movements in the light of Christian truth. It should seek
to counteract the influence of current propaganda, with its
deliberate distortion of truth and its sinister glorification
of war, by fostering a true understanding of peoples of
different racial and national background and by guiding
the energy of the members of churches into effective channels that may influence national policies in the direction of
peace. In lands where states, either as a result of conquest
or treaty or through mandates, govern subject peoples it is
incumbent upon the Christian churches to bear insistent
witness to the spiritual dangers inherent in this relationship and to insist that the welfare of those peoples is a sacred
trust to be exercised under the judgment of God. Public
administration in such countries should be directed toward preparing the people for a progressive share in the
affairs of government.

(f) *Disarmament.* The churches should constantly
warn their members of the grave danger involved in the
feverish and uncontrolled race for rearmament, as both a
symptom and a source of irresponsible power politics, and
should insist upon the need and practical possibility of limi-

ation and progressive reduction of armaments by confer-
nce and multilateral agreement.

(g) *Ecumenical Organization.*   We commend with
hankfulness the efforts of these movements which are work-
ng for the cause of international understanding through
he churches.   We rejoice in the decision taken by the con-
erence to recommend the creation of a world council of
hurches and we urge that the study of the problems dealt
vith in this report be included in its aims.

ADDITIONAL REPORT OF THE SECTION ON CHURCH AND COMMUNITY *

1. INTRODUCTION

THE CHRISTIAN church is called upon today to fulfill its mission amidst a distraught and disunited mankind. Divisions and conflicts within human society there have always been. But in the past these have been in the nature of tensions or strains, of varying intensity, within general frameworks of social unity which have persisted. In general the foundations of communal life in commonly accepted systems of customs, moral and cultural values and religious beliefs have remained firm. Today, as probably only once or twice before in human history, the foundations themselves are shaken. As a result, the corporate life of mankind has been thrown into confusion and disintegration and this social disunity is reflected in the lives of individual men and women, whose personal destiny is largely bound up with their relation to the community. Suffering, frustration and a baffled sense of the futility and meaninglessness of existence characterize personal living. Though

* This report was not submitted to the full conference. It is based on the original draft prepared before the conference and issued to all delegates. It has been largely rewritten in parts as a result of the discussions in the section. The general changes proposed in the original draft were submitted to the section at its final meeting. The section gave its general approval to the proposed changes and authorized the drafting committee to make the final revision. The main lines of the revised draft were discussed and settled in considerable detail by the committee and a good deal of the new matter, including the section on " Race," was approved in its present form by the committee. The task of final revision was entrusted to the chairman of the section and was completed after the conference.

more marked in some sections of mankind than in others, these facts are in some measure universal.

The vigorous attempts in many countries to restore social unity by drastic control and regimentation and by declaring national or class unity the supreme good, supreme over all else, only confirm this judgment. They bear witness to the primal need of human life for community and fellowship and to the tragic extent to which these have been lost in the present age.

In the midst of such a world, torn and disrupted and feverishly seeking a way out of its troubles, the Christian church stands and must fulfill its task. What is it to say? How is it to act? What is its understanding of the deeper meaning of the present situation of mankind? What, if any, is its wisdom for the healing of corporate disintegration and the restoration of sound and lasting community? What are individual Christians to believe and to do? It is with these questions that our report is concerned.

2. ANALYSIS OF THE EXISTING SITUATION

(a) *Social Disintegration.* The most general and the most significant phenomenon in the world of 1937 is the dissolution of the spiritual bonds and accepted organizing principles which have hitherto controlled and given meaning to the common life. This is due largely to the new ease of intercommunication among the peoples of the earth by train, steamer, airplane and telegraph. In particular, the shock of the impact of the West on the civilizations of the East and on the primitive peoples of Africa and Australia has been catastrophic. Everywhere men are brought into contact with whole peoples who do not share their unconscious assumptions and their habitual ways of feeling and acting. Their common customs are no longer carried on by the momentum of an unquestioned tradition. And, lately, the disintegration has been immensely speeded up by a cheap press and cheap literature, the cinema and the wireless. " The world has become a unity and for this high destiny mankind is not yet fit."

Another cause is the large-scale character of modern life. Thus, large-scale economic organization determines where and how vast masses of the population shall live. They quit villages for the great cities and are perpetually influencing and influenced by those with whom they have no personal contact. Owing to the size and complication of modern life, the major events are the total result of the pursuit by myriads of their own small, self-centered purposes. But no one has planned them as a whole and they come to the individual as fate. Personal responsibility is so widely diffused that it ceases to be felt.

These changes are not altogether evil. Often release from the control of tradition has opened the way for voluntary and purposeful associations with standards more intelligent and loyalties more vital just because they are freely chosen. This is particularly true of the growing emancipation of women. Thus the common man has been enabled to give freer play than before to his sympathies and to take a more active part in the molding of social conditions. Moral discipline may be the truer for being self-imposed.

But it is the sinister effects of the breakup of the old order of life that are more obvious. In many areas life and livelihood have become insecure through the menace of war and unemployment. Thus the unemployed man is uprooted. He no longer knows his place, for he has no clear function in the world in which he is no longer at home. His life has lost its meaning; he is frustrated and has no outlet for his normal energies. He has no clear direction for effort and no guarantee that effort is worth-while. He is typical in that he is abruptly called to live in a new and strange environment, adjustment to which may be the work of many generations.

Behind this physical insecurity lies a deeper spiritual insecurity. Everywhere the old standards of conduct are decaying because the convictions on which they rested have ceased to be held. The old loyalties and pieties have lost their unquestioned authority and no new ones have taken their place. Men are unstable, febrile, ill at ease, unsure of themselves or of how they want to live and what social obligations they will recognize. Thus the spiritual unity of the community is disturbed; for where no common standards can be assumed, men cannot trust or reckon on the actions of their neighbors. Both the individual and the community have " gone to pieces."

This disintegration is naturally most acute among the primitive peoples, especially those of Africa, on whom the impact of the West has fallen with shattering force, involving " the complete and rapid destruction of their spiritual and social and consequently of their moral life." But it is acute also in the East, and it is extensive in " Christendom," as is shown conspicuously in regard to the family. For centuries in the Christian West the rule of monogamy, though often broken in practice, was generally accepted in principle. Now, though the convention lingers, in very wide and apparently widening circles it has little moral reality behind it.

(b) *Contemporary Attempts to Reconstruct Social and Moral Life.* In many countries deliberate and sustained efforts are being made to take hold of and remold the common life. For Russian communism these efforts are based on complete devotion to a classless and equalitarian society that knows no national barriers. Corporate life is to be planned anew on severely rational principles. Impetus is derived from the exhilarating sense of a fresh start and the opening up of boundless possibilities. Sectional and national loyalties are to be entirely subordinated to the interest of the one overwhelming loyalty to the massed proletariat, and the rubbish of the past is to be cleared away to make room for a completely new building designed throughout for the purpose it is to fulfill. Equality and fraternity, if not liberty, are to be established and privilege is to disappear. All individuals or groups which stand in the way of the realization of this order are to be eliminated ruthlessly during the transitional period. Thus men are to master their destiny.

More commonly the nation is itself the basis of reconstruction. In Japan, China, India, Turkey, Egypt, Germany, Italy, Ireland and in many other countries, national patriotism is the dominant rallying and unifying force which wins the passionate devotion especially of the young. In these countries art and literature, manners, sport and physical culture take a strongly nationalistic color. The nation itself is recognized as the supreme object of devotion and therefore as the authoritative source of the established conventions of conduct which make possible an orderly social life.

Here, in contradiction to communism, the heritage of the past is highly prized. Modern nationalism is a deliberate revival of ancient loyalties and pieties. Alterations, if required at all, must be made " in the style of the building." The sense of continuity with a remote past and a remote future gives significance and dignity to the life of the present generation, which is aware of privilege in being the inheritor of a spiritual treasure of distinctive character and aware of responsibility for its unimpaired transmission to posterity.

If the evolution of society during the last few centuries

has been from corporate solidarity to individual self-determination, modern nationalism aims at a reversion to a position in which men's rights and duties spring naturally out of their station in the community. Instead of the individual's being solicited by a multitude of competing claims between which he himself has to arbitrate, the national community itself is to be the sole source of standards and values. The freedom of the individual to manage his own life as he will is deliberately sacrificed to social cohesion. That sacrifice is frequently voluntary and joyful because the freedom of the individual has too often proved to be a freedom of vacuity, like the " freedom " of the unemployed man to spend his time as he will. The individual surrenders his freedom gladly to the community which demands his uncritical obedience and loyalty but in return gives him an object in life and direction and the exhilaration of comradeship in the service of a common purpose.

Since man is more than mind and the nation is more than an association for definable purposes, the appeal of nationalism is made not only to the reason but to the whole man, including the emotions and the semiconscious springs of action. Liberal use is made of myth and symbol. As representative of the nation, the emperor in Japan and the Führer in Germany, like the " throne " in the British empire, are held in mystical veneration. A form of salute, a national anthem, a flag, the funeral of an " unknown warrior " are all used for the purpose of evoking enthusiasm. With this is connected the religious quality of the devotion, the absolute and unconditional character of the self-surrender to the nation, which has the intensity of devotion and self-sacrifice expected of a soldier in time of war and which is given with a faith that far transcends what can be justified on purely rational grounds.

Nationalism implies a concentration and its fraternity has clearly defined frontiers. It has often arisen in or been stimulated by a " war of liberation " in conscious opposition to foreign domination. After the World War, for instance, exhaustion and despair in the losing countries were commonly intensified by the crushing burdens of the peace treaties, and the resulting disintegration led to upheavals which were soul-stirring. The warmth of brotherhood felt among those who are within the circle is matched by the coldness or hostility toward those who are without. As with communism, there is ruthlessness toward individuals or groups who are obstacles to the closing of the ranks and there is a deliberate turning of the back upon cosmopolitan sympathies.

While nationalism has endeavored to revive ancient simplicities and pieties, it has been modern in its use toward that end of all the means of propaganda and mass suggestion made possible in recent years by science — press, cinema, wireless, etc. It has had great success in restoring vitality and confidence. Whether the reintegration effected has been on too narrow a basis and at the cost of disproportionate strains and stresses, it is too early yet to pronounce on empirical grounds.

(c) *The Seeming Exceptions.* The so-called democratic countries either did not participate in the World War or came out of it as victors. Naturally there have not been manifested in them such patent and vehement social convulsions as elsewhere and no such cataclysmic adjustments have followed. On the surface their social institutions and traditions exhibit a less radical breach of continuity. The current canons of individual and social behavior are in part derived from Christian sources and even when the theology that lay behind them has ceased to be generally believed, the old conception of the moral law and some of the old reverence for it still linger. Secularization has been less thorough and systematic than elsewhere.

But the difference has been one more of appearance than of reality. Here too the forces of dissolution are at work. The old standards are crumbling, especially for the younger generation; and even with the elders it is doubtful whether more than the outside of the cup and platter are really cleansed. The traditional way of life has no vital philosophy behind it. The great majority of those people who never enter a place of worship, and very many of those who do, hold with conviction neither the Christian nor any other Weltanschauung. Behind a façade of not entirely hypocritical conformity there are only confusion and half-beliefs. To a large extent this generation is living on its moral capital: it is living on the faith of its ancestors without having a faith of its own. It is drifting; and as in politics, so in regard to the whole order of community life, the initiative seems for the time to have passed to others. But here, too, before long, crucial decisions will have to be faced.

3. ITS CHALLENGE TO THE CHRISTIAN CHURCH

(a) *The Deeper Meaning of the Present Disintegration.* The church is under obligation to proclaim the truth that the disintegration of society has one fundamental cause. Men are at odds with themselves and with one another because they are at odds with their Maker. Mankind is sick primarily because, being made by and for God, they are doing violence to their own nature by striving to live without God. They ignore both his imperious claims and his gracious gifts. The only remedy for this sickness and the only genuine reintegration and possibility of true community lies in their return to God in whom alone is their peace and their well-being.

For several centuries the most dynamic forces in European civilization have been informed by a secularist revolt against the traditional Christian presuppositions on which the culture of Europe was founded. The original intention of this secularization in its most vital period was to establish a more genuinely universal community than Christianity had achieved. The elimination of religious bigotry and prejudice by disinterested intelligence was to make possible a universal culture and civilization based on generally accepted national standards of life and conduct. But in the event, this universalism has degenerated into an even more grievous particularism and parochialism than anything known in the Christian ages. European civilization is torn today by conflicts within and between nations through which the last vestiges of a common mind and common standards are being destroyed. Nations and classes are arrayed against one another, armed with world views and standards of conduct so incompatible that their common humanity is obscured and respect for one another denied.

This is the nemesis of an overestimate of the power and self-sufficiency of human reason. Secularists failed to take account of its finite and creaturely character and of the degree to which all its judgments are influenced by human interests and passions as well as by special historical circumstances and economic or biological conditions.

So man's supposedly universal judgments are discovered on inspection to be very particular and partial judgments derived from his own peculiar perspectives. But just because of their false claim to universality they become " demonic " [1] and give rise to monstrous spiritual pretensions

[1] " The demonic is something finite, something limited, which puts on infinite, unlimited dignity. Its demonic character is evident therein, that sooner or later another finite reality with the same claim will stand in opposition to it." (Tillich)

and fanatical fury against those who fail to share their habits, convictions and desires.

(b) *The Church's [2] Share in Responsibility for the Present Situation and its own Need for Repentance and Amendment.* Most lamentably the church's prophetic message to the world of today is discredited in advance. This is due not merely to the world's hardness of heart but to the church's own default. The modern situation is indeed God's call not only to the world but to a church which has been content to preach the redeeming word without the costly redeeming deed. This must be frankly recognized if that message is to be presented with any hope of carrying conviction.

What reason, for example, has the church given the world to believe that it has the secret of true community in him whom it preaches and professes to serve? The life of the church is deeply infected with the very ills from which humanity suffers. The divisions and conflicts of mankind have been reproduced and even justified within its borders. Again and again Christian groups have persecuted and sought to destroy one another and with equal guilt have persecuted men of other faiths — and this is still happening today. Thus a satanic element has entered the life of the church. A more genuine comradeship is sometimes to be found in non-Christian movements than in the Christian bodies.

Moreover, in relation to the modern world, the church has made one shameful and disastrous retreat. It has relied too exclusively on its priestly character and has tended to forget its prophetic mission. It has acquiesced in a situation in which religion is regarded as a specialized activity which

---

[2] By the " church " is here meant not the body of Christ — one, holy, catholic — but simply organized Christianity, that recognizable institution among other institutions whose doings the historian records.

does not and need not engage the interest of all and the gospel as simply the means of spiritual comfort for the individual. In large tracts of their lives Christians have failed to make their discipleship a reality; they have made clear neither to themselves nor to others the meaning of the gospel of redemption for the corporate life of mankind. Thus whether the church is treated outwardly with respect or with contempt it has ceased to affect vitally the lives of the larger part of the population even in the Christian West. It does not seem to them to have anything to say that is really relevant to the major interests and concerns. Thus the Christian religion is too commonly regarded neither with veneration nor with active hostility but with a tolerant indifference, as merely the hobby of those who happen to be inclined that way.

The root cause of the ineffectiveness of organized Christianity is the same as that of the present plight of the world, namely godlessness. But here it takes the more subtle form not of intentional denial or neglect of God but of taking his name in vain. Our basic failure has been a failure in wholehearted obedience and self-surrender to God, and this has been and is due to the insidious influence of individual and group egoism through which we mistake our own wills for the will of God and profanely invoke the name and authority of Christ in favor of prejudices and purposes that are all too human. The ultimate spiritual sin is to seek to use God instead of being used by him; and it is a sin to which all who undertake any enterprise in his name are constantly prone. Thus Christians have too easily identified — and have led the world to identify — the overlordship of God with the overlordship of the church, and it is in great measure their fault if the world's revolt, often largely justified, against the officers and members of the church has involved also a suicidal revolt against God.

Today, therefore, Christians are called to a new sincerity of surrender to God of all that they have and are, not excluding their own most cherished prepossessions. They must not approach the world with the righteous indignation and the conscious superiority of prophets whose unheeded warnings have now been proved true. Individually or corporately they can approach it with inward truth or with hope of conviction only if they do so as fellow prodigals who have indeed sinned more deeply in that they have sinned against the light, yet who have at last set their faces steadfastly to return to their father's house.

(c) *The Changed Relation of the Church to the Community.* This relation has had three main phases. The church originally came into the world as a tiny minority in the great Roman Empire. On the general community life of the ancient world, its manners and morals and institutions, the church of the catacombs could have no formative influence. Its only responsibility was for conforming or refusing to conform, for submission or for passive resistance. The second phase dates from the conversion of Constantine. A long process of permeation then began which culminated in the great conception of the *corpus Christianum*. A Christian world was envisaged based on a universal acceptance of Christian standards. All spheres of life were to be organized as a harmonious system under the domination of Christian standards and the supernatural guidance of the church.

But we are now living in a third phase. Since the Renaissance the secular order has gradually established its independence of ecclesiastical control. The church is no longer authoritative and dominant, it is only one among the many influences and movements of the modern world. Today convinced Christians are everywhere in a minority in a predominantly unchristian world. For the relation of the church to the community the mission field is now normative. The relation of the church in China to Chinese life is more typical than the relation of the church in Britain to British life; indeed the inner reality in Britain may be more like that in China than is commonly suspected. It is partly a sign and partly a cause of this change that large spheres of the common life, such as schools, universities and hospitals, in which for the Western world the church was once pioneer and controller, have been taken over for the most part by the community; and thus the church has lost much of its touch with the common life. It has lost channels of self-expression and of service to the community in which it could embody in deed and not merely preach in word something of the love of God.

The church has not yet faced the new situation with sufficient frankness. With the conservative instincts of all institutions of long standing and influence it has fought a defensive — and on the whole a losing — battle for the maintenance of as much as possible of the old ideal of the *corpus Christianum* and of the privileges and authority which that implies. But such a policy is doubly mistaken. First, it is quite unrealistic. The younger churches have never wielded such an authority, and for the older churches it is irrevocably gone — at least for the present era. Second, the ideal itself, though magnificent, was mistaken and premature. In practice it entailed more accommodation of the church to the world than of the world to the church. The present estrangement of the church from the world is not due only to the torpidity of Christians. It is indeed actually deepened by the outburst of new spiritual life in the church during the last hundred and fifty years as shown in the great missionary movements and in the quickened social conscience of Christians. For these make membership in the church more costly and mere conformity less attractive.

Thus the church finds itself today in a new relation to the community in which precedent is an insufficient guide. Domination it cannot have and possibly ought not to desire. Its present task is missionary even more than it is pastoral. In new circumstances it is challenged to find a new understanding of its duty to the common life. How far, for example, should it attempt to guide that life in regard to such matters as marriage, caste, the treatment of children and of animals? Amid the widespread disintegration, the appearance in many countries of new and active centers of moral and social authority on a secular and mostly on a nationalist basis, the survival in others of a somnolent semi-Christianity, and, on the other hand, the signs of a fresh stirring of the Spirit in the life of the church itself, what is the responsibility in each country of the Christian body?

(d) *The Challenge of the New Faiths.* In a time of spiritual chaos, the new faiths are vehement human endeavors to reintegrate life round a center. They evoke sentiments of loyalty, comradeship, self-discipline and self-sacrifice; and so far the church must welcome them.

But though communism and nationalism are utterly opposed to each other in their driving impulses and purposes, yet from a Christian standpoint they are exactly alike in one fundamental respect: they both constitute pseudo-religions. They claim to be the sole ultimate source and authority for the life of the individual and the community in all departments and they are resolutely bent on asserting this claim with ruthless intolerance and force. They put the classless society or the nation, its greatness and self-willed destiny, in the place of God. So they are essentially militant forms of idolatry because they claim for themselves what is due only to God, the Creator and Redeemer of all life. Such a claim can only be utterly repudiated and irreconcilably opposed by the Christian church in the name of God and for the sake of the whole human community it is called to serve. There is no hope in the ascription of sacred quality to nation or state or class. A false sacred, a false god, merely adds demonic power to the unredeemed passions of men. Though bringing about a temporary and local unity, it prepares for mankind an even worse and wider conflict. The church must call every individual or nation to obey God's will and live by his mercy. In no other way can a real reintegration be found.

Further, in so far as the community is cemented by the fostering of common antipathies, the new faiths challenge the second of the great Christian commandments. Such an attitude is incompatible with the Christian's duty to love his neighbor as himself. It is indeed the more unchristian when, in different countries, Negroes, outcastes, Jews or bourgeois are the objects of this antipathy on account not of any individual demerit but simply of their membership of a class. At the same time it is to be recognized that the appeal of the new faiths is often due to failures in organized Christianity itself. Christians have been guilty of dullness of heart, so that the oppressed have turned to others for help. The inertia and vagueness of the churches and their remoteness from the common life have often exhausted men's patience, so that they have turned from the way of Christ to the way of force. Hence these new religions challenge the church to face realistically, in the name of Christ's love, those social evils which others seek to abolish in violence and hate.

(e) *The Impersonal Character of Modern Life.* This challenge to the church is deeply affected by the predominance of the impersonal in modern life. In a world of social disintegration and of outer and inner insecurity in which men's hearts are failing them for fear the cry, " Save, Lord, or we perish," becomes insistent. It is more than individual faults and follies that have to be overcome. The social systems and institutions by which individuals are largely molded, indeed the whole framework of our lives, seem to have gone so awry that calamity and moral havoc are constantly being wrought by the sum of the actions of ordinary well meaning men. It is a question whether there is not a demonic element at work here and principalities and powers to be wrestled with. Human society's need for superhuman guidance and support is specially plain at this time.

But does the Christian gospel give any such guidance? Can any good thing come out of Nazareth? Has the simple Galilean world of direct personal relationships among a small number of friends and neighbors a message for the great society of today? If a man, loving God with all his heart and soul, is to love his neighbor as himself; if the Christian key to human living is the personal responsible, man-to-man (*Ich und Du*) relationship of brothers within the same Christian family — how is that to be applied in this world of large-scale organization, of complicated group relationships and of diffused responsibility? How is *das Gebot* to be obeyed in the existing *Ordnungen*?

4. THE CHRISTIAN POSITION ANALYZED

All Christian thinking about community must start from the church itself. The church is not just one more form of human gregariousness and association, one more attempt on the part of men to find a way of living together. It has come into being through God's gift of Jesus Christ as the Saviour of men in all their sinful impotence to find the true way of life. In the purpose of God it is the community of the followers of Christ redeemed by him and therefore called by him to be, since Pentecost, his witness and the chief instrument of his redeeming work in the world. It is thus itself God's special gift to men of community in spite of all the divisiveness of human selfishness. It is one body because it has one Head, and the life of the whole body and of every member is derived from communion with Christ. It is thus to be "a colony of heaven" in a fallen world, exemplifying by contrast the true way of human living; and its members are to be men inwardly constrained in loyal and thankful obedience to their Master to exhibit his spirit of sacrificial love in every sphere of their lives. Though in practice the institutional church has constantly belied this its essential character, the presupposition of all else that it attempts is that the church should really be the church. It can discharge its mission to the world only if it is continually renewing and deepening its own inner life in humble contrition and adoring gratitude.

(1) The General Impact of Christianity upon the Common Life

What duty has the Christian church toward the general social life of the world, its institutions, civilization and culture? Should Christians, individually and corporately, play a responsible part in this life? How far should they seek to remold it and on what principles? Amid the general chaos can or should the church seek to be a center of integration for the whole variegated and tumultuous life of the world? And what should be its relation to other partial centers of integration? What should be the impact of the church on the mass of traditions and prejudices, of unwritten codes and taboos by which in fact the community endeavors to direct its life — that is, the standards of decency, of what is done and what is not done, which most men actually apply in judging themselves and their fellows and by the gradual accumulation of which the normal routine of an orderly life has been formed? How far should it bless them and how far curse? In the background too are the rational systems which moral philosophers have tried to find underlying current moral practice and precept and providing at once a justification for them and a criterion for their further development. Of all these it is necessary to ask: What responsibilities have Christians in regard to them and what status or standards for criticizing them? And on what terms are Christians to live with their non-Christian or semi-Christian neighbors and to take part in the common life? These questions are perennial, but the answers have ever to be sought anew in a changing world. The special form which the question takes today is due to the general crumbling of traditional morality which in many circles seems to leave sincerity as the only virtue and hypocrisy as the only vice.

The answers will be much affected by the answers to certain theological questions: How far has God been at work, how far is his will to be discerned, in the development of civilization outside the immediate circle of the Christian church and the specific Christian revelation — in Greek ethics, in Roman law, in Teutonic ethos and institutions, in the traditional cultures and communal relationships of the ethnic religions, in the Oriental sense of the predominant importance of the things that are unseen, and in that which is more primitive and universal than them all, namely, the agelong traditional life of the tillers of the soil, their routine and simple pieties? How far are these things gifts of God or indirect revelations of him? All these questions are at once more urgent and more difficult when, as now, the secular order of life, its conventions and convictions, are themselves apparently in dissolution.

These questions must be asked, but the church is not yet in a position to give to them any clear and united answer. Before it can do so, a much more thoroughgoing and pro-

longed examination and interchange of ideals will be necessary. It is only possible now to prepare the ground for this
answer and to narrow down the area of uncertainty by indi-
cating certain governing principles.

First, Christ is the absolute Lord of all life. His sovereignty is not constitutional or limited or shared. His writ
does not cease to run " east of Suez " or in time of war or in
the complexities of modern civilization. His commandment is not merely a pathetic overstatement of principles
which are too easily ignored. He is not one among a number of prophets and we do not look for another. For the
Christian church the revelation of God in Jesus Christ is
finally authoritative in every department of life. Whatever authority conflicts with this is a usurpation. In the
sphere of practical life this is the fundamental principle
which is safeguarded by the orthodox assertion of the divinity of Christ.

But, second, though for Christians the gospel must
transcend and dominate, it does not supersede all ethical
knowledge and practice derived from other sources. In a
fully Christian world all the activities of life would be subjected to and judged by the gospel but not all would be
directly derived from it. God has created the whole world
and has been at work in it elsewhere than in consciously
Christian circles. Nowhere has he left himself without
witness, though that witness is distorted by human corruption. Thus in industry and commerce, art and literature,
sport and many other spheres of social life the bulk of the
legitimate aims and activities and of the common duties is
not directly derived from the Bible, but from secular traditions, professional codes, general reasoning, etc. For example, the creation of good music must be deemed to be in
accordance with God's will, yet good music does not mean
pious and edifying music but musical music. Such aims

and duties may well be recognized also by non-Christians and by halfhearted Christians; though for the Christian they are not absolute but are always subject to criticism and overruling in the light of the Christian gospel, and, in any case, it is the Christian gospel which will ultimately govern the ways in which these different activities are integrated in the lives of Christian individuals and communities.

Beyond this point Christians are still deeply divided. Toward the ways of living and standards of behavior approved by current social convention and adapted to the disciplining of " the average sensual man," some judge that as Christians they must be revolutionary in their attitude, others that as Christians they should in the main be acquiescent. This division is the chief hindrance to united Christian action in social life.

Large numbers of the most devoted Christians hold that the following of Christ, once undertaken, implies that agape, the essential Christian attitude, is to be the guiding principle in all relations of life. Christians therefore must not join or acquiesce in corporate action that is based on any lower principle. For the church to acquiesce in the exemption from the Christian law of love of any sphere of life in which Christians take an active part and to admit the validity of any such excuse, for instance, as hard economic or political necessity, would be to avow itself lacking in the one thing needful for discipleship. The duty of Christians is to strive to permeate society with Christian principles and so, God helping them, to make the kingdoms of this world the kingdom of God's Son. The tragic failure of Christendom has been that there has been so little attempt to apply really Christian principles to the common life on a large scale. As Chesterton says, " Christianity has not been tried and found wanting; it has been found difficult and not tried." The progress which has occurred has been due to a growing insight into the applicability of the exhortation, " Bear ye one another's burdens," to sphere after sphere of the common life. If, however, Christians cannot persuade society to adopt the Christian way, they will withdraw and live it out together. This is not necessarily to disclaim responsibility for the corporate life, since the truest public service may be rendered by the nonconformist.

But a section of Christians still larger numerically has always taken the opposite view. Of this second view there are two main forms. According to the first there is available a moral standard for the common life which is not the full commandment of the Christian gospel but has some relation to it and should very gradually approximate more nearly to it. This has been most fully worked out in the conception of " natural law " embodied in the Catholic tradition. Here is found a normative ideal for the common life, derived originally not from the Bible but from an analysis of secular institutions and standards combined with philosophic reflection. This gives at once a justification for existing conventions and codes, and a standard for their improvement. It is an ideal, but not a utopian ideal. It is a possible common basis for Christian and non-Christian; it embodies the virtues of justice and temperance but not of faith, hope and charity. Something similar is found in the conception of the " moral law " current in Anglo-Saxon countries. This was, in fact, derived largely from the Decalogue, but it was regarded as having validity independent of its theological origin, and so, in the eyes of all right-thinking persons, as having a claim to govern both private and public life. For Dr. Reinhold Niebuhr [3] the concep-

[3] Cf. his paper in the forthcoming volume, *The Christian Faith and the Common Life.*

tion of " justice " plays a somewhat similar part. To be willing to give other men their due and to be content with one's own due falls far short of Christian agape. But a world in which this principle was generally practiced would be a far better world than the present.

The second form of this view is based on a more radical pessimism. Here, too, the standards which govern the Christian in his intimate personal life are not regarded as applicable in the wider sphere of the common life, but for that there is no generally applicable moral standard. The whole complex of sentiment and implicit moral judgment and custom which actually governs the life of the community is to be regarded as part of the framework in which our lives are set by the ordinance of God. In their existing form these are far from " Christian," being largely the result of sin. Nevertheless, they serve by God's mercy to protect the human race, not indeed from sin itself, but from the ruin which is the natural result of sin; and they thus keep open the possibility of salvation though they cannot minister directly to it. They are dikes which keep out the flood, and the danger of chaos is so great that any order is better than none. Accordingly, ideals, as such, are untrustworthy. Human corruption infects so deeply all our efforts at betterment that we cannot take even gross evils as a sign that the social system of which they are an integral part must be mended or ended. The authority of the actual moral order in any community does not depend for Christians on its approximation to " natural law " or to any other moral standard — still less to the ideals of a sermon on the mount. The proper question is not, Does it approximate to the Christian law of love? (that is not to be expected anyhow; and the suggestion is only conceivable on the basis of a sentimental watering down of such sacrificial love into a mere general amiability), but, Does it help to avert the collapse of civilization? If so, its maintenance must be deemed to be in accordance with the sovereign will of God. Hence a modification of the existing order will be justified only if it springs out of the needs of the actual situation, and not on any general principle however " Christian."

Here is a radical division of principle between sincere Christians. It underlies and goes far to explain the notorious confusion and disunion concerning practical issues which give scandal to friends and enemies alike. It is inevitable that Christians should differ fundamentally as to what should be the church's attitude today toward war or the capitalist system or current penal law and practice or current sex morality, when there is no agreement between them about the standards by which they are to judge. Some differences of application there will always be, but differences of principle of such magnitude are stultifying.

There is urgent need that these differences be further explored and that Christians make an earnest and sustained effort to reach a more common mind.

(2) The Duty of Christian Individuals and Groups within the Common Life. The Problem of Personal Compromise

Over against the world at large the Christian is bound to a distinctive way of life. He is to love God with all his heart and soul and, therefore, to love his neighbor as himself. He is to give his brethren not merely their due but an unconditional love and service; and this Christian agape is qualitatively different from any natural affection or any rational benevolence which implies reciprocity. He attaches an absolute value to his neighbor, not as being such and such, more or less likable or more or less virtuous, but simply as a fellow man and therefore a child of God, and there, like himself, one of those for whom Christ died. This attitude can only be justified on the basis of faith and not of any empirical evidence. It is based on the redemptive love of God for men revealed in the life and death of Jesus Christ. The gospel has set forth the family as the regulative standard of human relationships — but the family as it is not in quiet times but when it has survived triumphantly the highest imaginable tension, when its members are awake with a quivering sensitiveness to all that it means. To exemplify this spirit to the best of its ability is incumbent on a sincerely Christian community — for example, a Christian household — and through the grace of God it has been exemplified in some degree, if only fitfully, in saintly lives in every generation.

In the past, Christians in general have in effect established a working compromise with the moral standards of the surrounding society. Through the influence of the Christian conscience some flagrant wrongs have disappeared from the world or have been greatly reduced. There is, for instance, more consideration for women and children, for the aged and sick, and for the poor and needy. The general conscience of civilized society has been roused to some genuine understanding that men are their brothers' keepers. But to a larger extent Christian people, in their ordinary weekday life in the world, have adopted the current standards of contemporary respectable society rather than made an independent Christian contribution to them. The Christian layman in a " Christian " country mixing with others in his home, in the workshop or the office, in the public house or on the golf links, has recourse to the generally accepted standards which he himself commonly shares. Some of these are general, such as the ideals of the " gentleman," the " sportsman," the " good pal," the " man of honor "; others are professional and specialized, such as the

" good workman," the " upright businessman," the " just judge," the " chivalrous warrior." The distinctive, devoted, unworldly aspect of the Christian life has fallen into the background here, even with those to whom it is a reality in their more intimate and personal relations. When in Rome they not only do as Rome does, but they do it for much the same reasons as others. They strive to make a living at the expense of their competitors, they go to the law courts to defend their rights and they provide for a rainy day rather than give all their goods to the poor. The only exceptions are specialists, like monks and nuns, or minorities of peculiar people, like the " sects."

Is all such compromise an unworthy backsliding, a sign of unfaithfulness and disloyalty for which penitence is due? If so, the practice of Christianity on a large scale has never yet been attempted, and that may be the chief cause of the present plight both of the world and of the church. Or is it a genuine obedience to the spirit rather than to the letter and a sign of a sane realism as opposed to a sentimental utopianism?

On this issue sincere Christians today are deeply divided, and while that division lasts there can be little unity on practical policies. To obtain further light and — D. V. — more of a common mind upon it is of the most urgent importance for the whole church. For the world as a whole today, and even in " Christian " countries, the church has little vital impact on the common life as a whole. This is largely due to a pervading sense of unreality which affects both the reaction of the world to the church and the mind of the church itself. When the church adapts itself to current standards the world feels that — consciously or unconsciously — Christians are hypocrites; they do not really believe what they preach, for they don't attempt to practice it. On the other hand, with the more uncompromising

Christians the world feels that these are brave words but quite unrealistic, and that their utterers belong to that type of idealist in whom the wish to believe is paramount, who will not face realities and who is forever deceiving himself with beautiful dreams. And in both cases the Christians in their hearts feel something of this themselves, and their spiritual power and effectiveness are fatally weakened by unconfessed and only half-conscious misgivings. Before all things it is necessary that the Christian message for the common life regain " the bracing sense of effective reality."

On the one view conscious compromise is inconsistent with any sincerity of discipleship. Christ's commandment is, " Be ye perfect, as your Father in heaven is perfect." Nothing less than absolute purity, absolute honesty, absolute agape in all circumstances is to be the Christian's aim. The Christian knows in advance that, being faulty and erring, he will not achieve it; but to *aim* at less is to betray his Master. Moreover, it is faithless to speak and act as if his possibilities were limited by his own strength: if his surrender is wholehearted he has the grace of God on which to rely. To prudential arguments about consequences he is deaf; consequences are not his responsibility; they are not in his hands but in the hands of God. Also, he will be on his guard against the immense temptation to self-deception. In nothing is the corruption of human nature more manifest than in the plausible sophistries by which we seek to persuade ourselves that the line of least resistance can be justified on the highest moral grounds. To such arguments the Christian reply is simple — " Get thee behind me, Satan."

On the other view there are various limitations which make impossible any direct application of the principle of redemptive love as revealed in Jesus Christ to the whole field of the common life. First, human individuals or groups are finite, and therefore can dispose of only a limited amount of time and attention and active sympathy. In Christ the love that beareth all things, believeth all things, hopeth all things, endureth all things, was extended to all mankind. With men it is possible at best toward a very few. Not only through moral defect, but in the nature of the case, it cannot be the guiding principle of our action toward the majority of those with whom we have dealings. Second, if there is to be common action between any large number of persons, that implies a formula of some sort. But any formula or program or " rule of life " for a group must fall below the level of the spontaneous action of its best members; for such action — action for example in the spirit of I Corinthians 13 — arises not in obedience to any rule but as the irresistible welling up of spontaneous feeling. It is no more explicable by a rule than the highest achievements of artistic genius are explicable by any conceivable esthetic formula. Third, for joint action between Christian and non-Christian there is a further limitation. (It is hardly possible to avoid such joint action altogether; and any avoidance which is less than total is more effective for quieting uneasy Christian consciences than for affording real relief from responsibility for the common life.) Social rules which are to bind non-Christians and semi-Christians as well as the converted, and which require their concurrence if they are to be effective, can only prescribe the highest standard for which the communal mind is yet ripe; for it is necessary to reckon not only with opinions which can be changed fairly quickly, but with ingrained assumptions and sentiments which control the routine of life and are only very gradually alterable. The justification for such participation is that " half a loaf is better than no bread." It is certainly the Christian's duty in every situation to do what is God's will for him in that situation; there can be no compromise there. But it may be God's will for him to do in that situation what regarded in the abstract would be sub-Christian.

To the problem of compromise, which has perplexed and harassed the soul of every sincere Christian since Christ's day, there is no clear and simple solution. Quite possibly God's will in this matter varies for each person; it is known only to God, and it is revealed only to the individual as he seeks penitently and earnestly to open his mind to the guidance of the Spirit. Nevertheless one or two general statements can be made.

Through all the Christian centuries there have been within the life and leadership of the church representatives of each of the two main alternative positions, whom their fellows and the judgment of subsequent generations have recognized as true and devoted followers of Christ. The distinction between the " sect " and the " church " types of practical Christianity appears clearly in the earliest records of the primitive church itself, and it corresponds in some measure with the distinction of prophet and priest in the ministry of the church. The stubborn persistence and constant recurrence of these two views of the Christian life and types of Christian fellowship and worship suggests that both have their necessary place within the wider reality of Christ's church. The exclusive predominance of the one would produce an irresponsible individualism and would destroy continuity; the exclusive predominance of the other would produce a stagnant conformity and would prevent advance.

Again, men's natural attraction is to conformity; there is an inherent lag and drag in human nature which is part of man's sinfulness. Therefore every man must be warned unremittingly of this incurable tendency and be put on his guard against it. Further, it is the prophets who pioneer mankind's advance — almost always at the price of misunderstanding and abuse, often at the cost of persecution and martyrdom. The blood of the martyrs is the life of the church. Therefore the church and every Christian owe a special duty of sympathy and support to fearless and devoted pioneers.

But " compromise " is an ambiguous term. If Christians would think clearly about their own lives or fairly about their fellows, they must recognize the clear distinction between conduct due to the limitations which are implicit in human finiteness and in the given conditions of social life (which is often misleadingly called " compromise "), and true and blameworthy compromise which implies a failure to fulfill genuine possibilities of faithful discipleship. To recognize this distinction is not to relax the moral tension by justifying sin. There is enough undeniable sinful compromise in every man's life to bring the honest spirit to despair. But to call that sin which is really part of God's structure for life is to falsify truth. Like every other form of exaggerated self-mortification it leads either to unhealthy morbidity or inverted self-righteousness through unnatural self-concern.

Yet here too the temptation to self-deception is great. There is no such thing as a life without compromise, not only in the legitimate sense of adaptation to given conditions but also in the deeper and sinful sense of avoidable failure in faithful discipleship. There is in all our acts some wrongful shortcoming which only a pharisaic legalism can ignore. Every sensitive Christian knows well enough that he is so failing at every moment; he is always a sinner. At all times we must confess, " We are unprofitable servants."

(3) The Church and Community

(a) *Community and "the Orders."* The church discovers each person, never as an isolated individual, but always enmeshed in a web of organic corporate relationships which surround his life in concentric circles of ever widening radius — his family, his neighborhood, his race, his people, his nation, all humanity. To these powerful organic structures or relationships which are continuing features of human life in every age and among all peoples the Germans give the name *die Ordnungen,* " the orders "; their nature and their true significance in the Christian understanding of life is one of the most disputed issues in contemporary Christian thought.

Each relationship conditions and molds both the life and the thought of every person in greater or less measure, usually in more subtle and pervasive ways than he realizes. Each makes invaluable contributions to his existence, and in return lays upon him obligations to loyalty and service. For Christian faith, each in its true expression is, in some sense, a part of the divine order, part of God's gracious provision for the enrichment of man's life. But there is conflict between their respective claims. Much more important for Christian faith, each is forever tending to make demands upon the Christian in conflict with his duty to God. Like every individual, each of the great corporate societies or " orders " of human life is always infected with the sins of pride, fear, idolatry, greed and insularity. They are always partly God-inspired, partly sin-infected and therefore " demonic " in their claims. In consequence, the life of each Christian is *always* in tension between the illegitimate demands (usually exaggerations or perversions of legitimate demands) of the various " orders " upon him and the demand which alone rightly claims his unqualified devotion — that of the will of God. Hence spring many of the most perplexing problems of the Christian's life in the world.

The most intimate and meaningful of these societies or "orders," and much the most rightful in its demands, is that of *family*, for to it each person owes not only his very existence but all the gifts of early nurture and protection. Its ties are biological, not merely cultural or historical or accidental or sentimental. Indeed so universal is the recognition of the profound claims of family that each of the wider societies or " orders " seeks to appropriate for its own claims the same advantage by presenting itself to men as the " larger family." Thus members of lodges, fraternities, clans and nations, as well as churches, call each other " brother " and " sister " in their efforts to lay upon the individual the obligations of family loyalty. Yet the demands of the family itself may be, and often are, in unresolvable conflict with duty to God and therefore " demonic." Hence Jesus' stringent injunction, " Unless ye hate father and mother and wife and children and brothers and sisters, ye cannot be my disciples." (Luke 14:26)

The relationship or " order " next after family in the enrichment of the individual and his consequent loyalty to it may be the *neighborhood* in which he dwells, or a particular *society* or *organization* or *communion* of which he is a member. (For, as a human institution, the church is one society or " order " among others, making its contribution and claiming its loyalty as they do, and like them forever in danger of infection by sin, thus becoming " demonic.") Or, the society or " order " of next strongest claim may be the individual's *people* or *nation*, or even *humanity*. In any event, these latter and wider corporate realities each make their contribution to him and lay their claim upon him — the people or folk to whom his life is bound by profound ties of common heritage, custom, experience and, it may be, blood; the nation-state of his residence; the race of his birth; and the great body of mankind which the Christian by faith recognizes as the company of the sons and daughters of God — his Father's family upon earth.

It is in the relative importance of these societies or " orders," in the legitimate or " demonic " character of their respective claims, and especially in the true relation between his duty to them and his sovereign duty to God that many of the Christian's most poignant perplexities lie. It is here that some of the most serious misunderstandings among Christians today arise.

The difficulty is intensified because there is no single set of terms by which the different relationships or " orders " are uniformly understood in different parts of the world. But that is not merely a defect of language. The difficulty in language is a revelation of the problem, not its cause. It is due to the deeper fact that the relationship which each of these terms designates and which is set forth in its dictionary definition has markedly different meanings and associations in different parts of the world. And, since the practical reality is not the abstract relationship, but the *meaning* of the relationship — the actual grip which it has upon whole peoples — we have to do not merely with confusion of terms but with different realities. Therefore it must be recognized first that none of the most familiar terms — community, nation, people, *Volk*, race — , various forms of which are frequently employed interchangeably, are precise equivalents. Second and more important, it must be recognized that *each* of these terms is differently understood by different sets of people and *means* different things to them. It is these various meanings which must be understood if discussion is to be fruitful.

For example, each of these wider corporate realities — neighborhood, organization, church, people, nation, race, humanity — may be designated as a *community*. But concerning their relative significance as *communities* there is wide difference of view. Thus a European writer defines a *community* by contrast with an *association*. An association may be defined by the purpose for which it is constituted. It is formed for particular ends such as trade, recreation, study, mutual security. As a rule its membership is voluntary; an individual may disassociate himself from one association and join himself to another. But a *community* is a corporate reality of a very different kind. It is the whole of a people living continuously together in one area when, as such, they share a common social life and form. It is something to which one is born, not something which one chooses to join. Its ties are those of historic origin, not those of pragmatic usefulness. It is a natural growth rather than an artificial creation. Its purposes are too many and too indefinite to be enumerated and all of them together do not fully explain its existence or its character. Its cohesion is largely subconscious and semi-instinctive and it is more lasting than that of an association. Its fellow feeling and the purposes it subserves are not the cause of its members' living together but rather flow out of that.

Yet there is not a single element in that definition of " community " which is not refuted by corporate realities in various parts of the world which are undoubtedly communities. In the United States, the most frequent meaning of " community " is not " the whole of a people," but " a segment of the people living in geographical proximity," a neighborhood. The Jewish people do not " live continuously together in one area " but are scattered over the face of the earth, yet feel themselves one community; and the same might be said of the British empire. The Swiss national community shares several languages and cultures. The American people is a community into which many of its members were not born but which they chose to join; its ties are less those of historic origin than of pragmatic usefulness. Many modern nations with a deep sense of community are less " natural growths " than " artificial creations." Of some of them it must be said that " its fellow feeling and the purposes it subserves *are* the cause of its members' living together," and not the reverse. For increasing numbers of Christians, the *Christian world community* which possesses no geographical locus, no tangible structure, no unity of language or uniformity of custom, is a reality of far greater meaning and authority than the innumerable local, racial and national communities which have traditionally claimed human devotion.

In brief, the one essential condition of a community is that its members should feel themselves to be a social whole, that is, that they should feel themselves to be a community. For community, the reality is constituted by profound awareness of common interest or affection or loyalty or aspiration and not by factors of racial kinship, historic association, geographical propinquity or shared experience. The latter may be precedent; they may be derivative; they may be nonexistent.

Much the same thing may be said of the inner realities which bind a people together into a *nation* and which quicken the consciousness of obligation and debtorship. In the United States, where unity proceeds from no identity of race or blood, no long historic continuity of life and custom, no great body of common folkways, but from a common ideal rather than a common history, it is the nation-state to which loyalty adheres. In central and eastern European countries, in recent years especially, there has been a mighty resurgence of loyalty to *Volk* (a term for which there is no precise English equivalent, the closest parallel being perhaps " people ") , loyalty to the corporate reality to which one belongs by deep historic association and racial kinship, by which the heritage of the past is continued and the common life sustained, and which, it is maintained, is the " order " established by God next in importance to *family* for the nurture and discipline of man.   In Great Britain loyalty is given to " king and country " — a reality intermediate between the American nation-state and the continental *Volk*.   And there are other variations among other peoples.   Here, likewise, a nation is a nation because its members feel themselves to be so and, consciously or implicitly, are resolved to remain so.

Again, with regard to the hold which national ties take upon the loyalties of members, there is the widest diversity. At one end of the scale are peoples in whom the rebirth of the sense of nationality has lately come as a profound and shattering vital experience to which all else must be related, like a volcanic eruption in whose glow the whole landscape is lit up.   At the other is the people of the United States, which is and feels itself a nation but has no single common blood, language or culture and for which a common soil is only a recent acquisition.   Again, for a Frenchman himself, and for understanding him, it is obviously far more important that he is a Frenchman than that he is a Gascon or a European.   With a Briton, it is less obvious whether it is more significant and matters more that he is British or that he is Scottish, Welsh or English.   With a French Canadian it is far from clear whether he is primarily French, Canadian, British or American; and with a recent immigrant from Europe to the United States, whether it is his old or his new nation to which he most belongs.

(b) *The Church and National Community (Volk)*. The problem of *community* is given a special setting and urgency at the present time by the crucially central place which the reality of *Volk* has come to have in the thinking of many peoples, especially the German-speaking peoples of the continent of Europe. It must be clearly grasped that the word *Volk* is, strictly speaking, quite untranslatable into English just because it designates both a sentiment and a body of convictions to which there is no exact or even approximate parallel elsewhere. (The Japanese philosophy and practice of emperor worship reveals analogies to political nationalism but not to the sentiment of *Volk*. The British sentiment toward the crown has points of kinship but is supported by no such mythical and metaphysical structure.) As Professor Ernest Barker writes:

Our word " community " is a multicolored word. It has many areas of operation. The German word *Volk* is a unitary word. There is one *Volk,* though it may have two different manifestations according as we are thinking of the *Volk* already included in the boundaries of the German state or of the broader *Volk* which transcends those boundaries. . . . None of us can use the word " community " with the simple intensity with which the German uses the word *Volk*. When we think of the realities of church and community, we are thus thinking of something different from the relation of *Kirche* and *Volk*.

Because of its great importance for Europeans today, Christians everywhere should make special efforts to come into an understanding of the inner meaning of *Volk*. It is thus described by a competent authority:

Volk is not an institution, but a living personal community of a superindividual kind. The elements by which it is constituted, viz. identity of blood, occupancy of the same territory, possession of the same language, customs, history and culture, etc., are of different strength at different times. *Volk* is best understood on the analogy of the family. It stands for common descent in the spiritual and physical sense of the word. It has to be distinguished from society, class, mass, nation and state. It is not a sum of individuals, or a collective compound, but as it were a living being of community life. *Nation* means *Volk* or the population viewed in its political aspect. Fascism takes the concept of *Volk* under its political aspect. The German conceives the *state* as the instrument to form and keep the people a continuing and growing force. *Volk* is an organic thing; *state* an organization.

Although this recrudescence of passionate loyalty to *Volk* seems to many people today a new and strange phenomenon, it has its roots deep in history, indeed in Christian history. It has been a central issue in the relations of church and community for fifteen centuries. It first presented itself as a problem for Christian thought and life when missionaries carried Christianity to the barbarian tribes of northern Europe in the fifth and following centuries. Though, through Judaism, Christianity itself had tribal and national affiliations, it had grown up under the Roman Empire and had shaped itself in a world imbued with imperial culture and presuppositions. But the empire was breaking up, and the barbarians already had their own tribal religions, linked with all phases of the common life of the tribe. To a large extent the missionaries adapted themselves to this pattern and Christianity was domesticated to tribal and national loyalties. Since that day the life of the church has reflected the tension in Europe between imperial and national ideals, between the relatively rational, civilized and sophisticated ideals of *homo sapiens* and the more primitive, intimate unreflective group loyalties of the natural man. The Reformation marked the triumph of nationalism in the sixteenth and seventeenth centuries. In the eighteenth and nineteenth centuries, under the influence of rationalism and humanitarianism in the secular world and of the missionary movement and the ideal of the world-wide community of Christians in religion, the intense and exclusive ties of national loyalty were somewhat relaxed in favor of universalism in both politics and religion. Today they are again clamant.

Thus the true place of national or community or *Volk* loyalty in the life of the Christian, and the true relation of the Christian church to these natural and powerful societies, has been a mooted but unsettled issue throughout the greater part of Christian history.   We here confront not merely the personal problem of conflict between claims of community and duty to God.   There is the far deeper issue of the place which these " orders " or societies are believed to hold in God's wider purpose for all mankind.   In this matter Christians are not fully agreed.   But there is unanimity as to the following basic principles.

The Christian attitude toward national community or *Volk* must depend in the first instance on the place Christians assign to it in the divine economy.   The starting point is the double recognition already noted — nation or *Volk* is always at once both God-given and sin-infected.   The Christian is called upon to accept and rejoice in the fact that God has chosen to set men in various races, peoples and nations, with different manners and styles of life.   That each nation seems to have its distinctive contribution and mission to the world is to be ascribed to God's purpose.   The ties of common blood, soil, tradition, culture and purpose which constitute the national community are by nature enormously strong.   They are given of God who creates the individual life in and through the life of a specific community.

On the other hand, it must be said with the greatest emphasis that, as with every divine gift, the gift of nation has been and is being abused by men and made to serve sin. Any form of national egotism whereby the love of one's own people leads to the suppression of other nationalities or minorities, or to failure to respect and appreciate the gifts of other people, is sin and rebellion against God who is the Creator and Lord of all peoples.   The history of every nation is defaced by national crimes; every nation has its distinctive national defects as well as its distinctive excellences. More fundamental still, even the best things in national life have in them an element of sinful self-assertion and self-glorification, of indifference and contempt for " the lesser breeds without the law " and of the will to lord it over them. Everywhere in the life of nations and peoples these two elements have been and are at work; it is not possible to disentangle them and to say with confidence, " This is the work of God " and, " This is the work of the devil." But to see in one's own nation the source and standard of revelation, or in any other way to give the nation divine status, is utterly sinful.

Thus the Christian attitude toward nation or *Volk* will be twofold. The primary call on the loyalty and service of both the church and the individual believer is as a rule to the community in which God has set them. The love of the Christian for his people should be part of his gratitude to God for the riches which are his through the community into which he has been born. Each generation has inherited from the past a distinctive ethos and culture by which its own mind and character have been shaped. Of this it is a trustee rather than an owner. It is its duty to preserve that inheritance and to transmit it unimpaired and if possible enhanced to posterity. Every church should regard itself as a church for the whole people, not in the sense that it would subordinate itself to the national life but in the sense that it accepts its place in the community and acknowledges its responsibility, along with all other Christian bodies, to reach all members of the community with the Christian message.

But the obligation both of Christian and church is rather to loyalty than to obedience or conformity — and loyalty itself sometimes requires vigorous opposition to the general will. The prophets of Israel constantly withstood, rebuked and prophesied against their own people and their constituted authorities; that is why they were stoned. In doing so they transgressed no patriotic duty. Rather, they themselves were the true patriots because they spoke and acted not in " abject submission " to the " occasional will " of their nation but out of a deep and true insight into the things that belonged to its peace. So, likewise, Jesus spoke out against the evils in national and *Volk* life in sharp and unsparing denunciation. While the Christian church in any country consists predominantly of the members of the people of that country, it has a unique character in that it is based on conscious allegiance to God in Christ and its center is beyond this world. It has its own distinctive task of witness and worship which for its members constitutes an imperative transcending all others. To submit to interference in its performance would be apostasy; it would be to obey man rather than God. In addition, it can view folkways and national claims from a perspective unavailable to others, in the light of the knowledge of God in Jesus Christ, and it must maintain thereby a prophetic and critical outlook upon the national life as a whole. More particularly, where nation or *Volk* is deified or made supreme over all other peoples and all other claims this pretension must be utterly repudiated and irreconcilably opposed both by the individual Christian conscience and by the Christian church in the name of God. Further, the church is called to be watchful that such sinful pretensions, or the world views by which they are supported, do not enter within its own life, destroying its supernational fellowship and corrupting the pure word of the gospel which it is called upon to preach.

Thus far all Christians may agree. To this extent they may, and should, present a united and powerful witness concerning both the positive validity and the " demonic " pretensions of the claims of nation or *Volk*. But beyond this large and important area of agreement there are serious differences of conviction. As we have noted, they have their roots far back in history. And they cannot be said to arise wholly from theological divergences as to the place of nation or *Volk* in the divine economy. It is only too apparent that, through the whole of Christian history and not least today, they have been strongly colored by political exigencies and loyalties; Christians have tended to favor that view of the divine significance of nation and *Volk* which most readily supported the political interests of their own people.

To some, it appears that national community or *Volk*, like the family to which it is akin and to which it stands next in the divine economy, is an order especially created by God for the preservation of the heritage of the past, the nurture and training of the successive generations and the maintenance and improvement of the common life of men. Any weakening of its demands upon individual loyalty and obedience is a blow not only to social stability but to the very structure of morality and religion. Duty to *Volk* is in the last analysis duty to God; its claim upon persons is well-nigh absolute. To others, it seems that the semi-instinctive and subrational emotions of *Volk* loyalty come down from primitive and precivilized levels; they appeal to all that is parochial, bigoted and fearful in man and their continuance is a device of conservative forces to preserve the status quo and block progress. A radical emancipation from their hold upon individual sentiment and obedience is essential for growth into the wider and more inclusive loyalty to the body of humanity. Excessive deference to *Volk* is in the last analysis apostasy to God who, as Father of all mankind, intends every person to come into the reality of the universal brotherhood of his children. The central issue is thus clear. It is the relation in the divine plan of loyalty to the narrower but more intimate and intense bonds of community or *Volk,* to the wider but more general loyalty to the whole family of God's children. Is that more limited loyalty God's special provision for human nurture and discipline — next to the family in legitimate obligation — or is it a persistence of tribal feeling from which men should be freed in order to realize the divine commonwealth? Is that wider loyalty merely an abstract humanitarianism masquerading under Christian aegis, or is it the ultimate fellowship toward which God ever seeks to lead his unwilling children? This is an issue urgently requiring concerted Christian study.

(c) *The Church and Race.* A special problem of critical urgency today is that of the relations between peoples of different races. Here all of the deep human loyalties and prejudices which are present in both lofty and demonic form in all phases of the common life — pride in ancestry and heritage, dislike of alien peoples and unfamiliar ways, tension between more advanced and less advanced cultures, fear of contamination and desire for opportunity, economic greed and economic need — come to most extreme and dangerous expression. And there are in addition deep-seated antipathies and apprehensions peculiar to race relationships. The roots of the problem are deep and difficult of treatment. No simple or easy solution is possible. It is all the more imperative that Christians have a clear and firm grasp of the Christian truth concerning race, the nature of the present situation and the Christian's responsibility for action.

For Christians, the starting point in this as in every problem of the relations of men is the affirmation that all men are by birthright children of God created in his image, and therefore brothers and sisters to one another. They are, moreover, " brothers for whom Christ died," and are intended by God to be brought within the fellowship of his one true church.

Each of the races of mankind has been blessed by God with distinctive and unique gifts. Each has made, and seems destined to continue to make, distinctive and unique contributions to the enrichment of mankind. All share alike in the love, the concern and the compassion of God. Therefore, for a Christian there can be no such thing as despising another race or a member of another race. Moreover, when God chose to reveal himself in human form, the Word became flesh in One of a race then as now widely despised. Christ himself selected as the supreme illustration of the charity he enjoined upon his followers a member of a hated and outcast people — outcast because they were of mixed blood (the good Samaritan). For Christians, alien or outcast peoples claim special regard.

Each race is rightly grateful for its own heritage and possibilities. Apparently, each desires to preserve its own identity. What it chiefly desires of other races is not opportunity for intermarriage, but recognition of its dignity within the family of mankind and opportunities for education, for significant vocation and for social intercourse within the common life. As to the desirability or undesirability of widespread admixture of races, the authorities are sharply divided. This is a matter to which Christian and scientists should give determined study. It must be noted, however, that such mixture of less advanced and more advanced peoples as has occurred has been mainly due to the initiative and often to the violence or fraud of the latter. Further, there is today, apart from certain primitive peoples, no such thing as a " pure race." The assumption by any race or nation of supreme blood or destiny must be emphatically denied by Christians as without foundation in fact and wholly alien to the heart of the gospel.

The problem of the relations of the races is found today chiefly in two situations: within a nation where large numbers of two or more races dwell together and between nations of different races. In either situation, the problem may arise between races of relatively equal culture or between markedly more and less advanced peoples. It is to be noted that the problem *within* nations is most acute where, as in North America, the minority were first introduced into a country by violence and at the instance and solely for the benefit of the people which now denies them social equality; or, as in many parts of Africa, Asia and Australasia, where the dominant people themselves are an alien minority in a land originally belonging to those whom they now dominate; or, as in the case of the Jewish nation, of a people forcibly exiled from their homeland who were originally often welcomed for what they could contribute to the dominant nation's welfare. In the first two instances especially the predominant motive was economic exploitation and aggrandizement. In brief, the most acute situations today are largely due to movements of population initiated by white and so-called " Christian " nations for their own advantage. Individual Christians and their churches bear a heavy guilt.

The gravity of the problem cannot be exaggerated. Both within certain nations and on the wider scale of the world-wide relations of the races, catastrophe is hardly to be avoided without clear-sighted and courageous action. It seems doubtful if it can be avoided in any event except through the wisdom and power of religion. In this task, the Christian church is called to play a major, it may be a decisive, part; and every Christian has a twofold responsibility — as a citizen and as a member of the church of Christ.

The concrete forms of the problem vary widely in different communities and lands. There is no single or simple solution. But there are certain principles which Christians everywhere should seek to have incorporated in the sentiments and public policies of their nations and communities. Among these are:

(1) The recognition of the value of every human being as a person.

(2) The right of every person, whatever his race, color or present status, to the conditions essential for life as a person; to education; to opportunity in his vocation, recreation and social intercourse.

(3) Full participation in fellowship and leadership for members of a less advanced people as they prove their ability.

(4) Active cooperation and fellowship among leaders of different racial groups.

(5) Recognition by the community of its responsibility to less privileged persons of whatever race or group, not only for their assistance and protection but also for special educational and cultural opportunities.

(6) The necessity of such economic and social change as shall open the way to full opportunity for persons of all races.

However, it is as members of the church of Christ that Christians bear the heaviest guilt for the present situation. And here is their greatest obligation and opportunity:

The first need is that the deepest inner attitude of every Christian toward persons of other races be completely transformed by the gracious gift of God into conformity with the mind of Christ. Persons of all races should become to the Christian sons and daughters of God, differing in color, in native endowment, in custom and outlook, but of one brotherhood in God's love and so, by God's grace, in the affection of the Christian. It is a standing rebuke to Christians that this attitude has in fact been more fully realized in some secular and non-Christian movements than within the churches. Such an inner transformation is to many Christians one of the richest gifts of God in which they greatly rejoice. It is a gift which every Christian should possess and which God waits to bestow on all who will receive it.

In the second place, Christian congregations are infected in their attitudes and practices by the same prejudices, fears, distortions of truth and exclusions as those which create the race problem in the secular community. But it is a first responsibility of the Christian church to demonstrate within its own fellowship the reality of community as God intends it. It is commissioned to call all men into the church, into a divine society that transcends all national and racial limitations and divisions. In its services of public worship, in its more informal fellowship and in its organizaton, there can be no place on any pretext whatever for exclusion or compulsory segregation because of race or color. " In Christ there is neither Greek nor Jew, barbarian nor Scythian, bond nor free." The congregation or communion which allows its line of action to be determined by such racial discrimination denies the gospel whose proclamation is its task and commission.

Third, in the Christian home there can be no barriers or discriminations because of race, color or social status. It is to be recognized that such a course may involve difficulties and raise apprehensions lest such intimate social intercourse lead to unwise marriages which would impose unfair handicaps on later generations. Yet with all its difficulties it will be gladly undertaken by the Christian in confident loyalty to the free and gracious fellowship of Christ's brethren.

Fourth, against racial pride, racial hatreds and persecu-

tions and the exploitation of other races in all their forms,
the church is called by God to set its face implacably and
to utter its word unequivocally both within and without its
own borders.   There is special need at this time that the
church throughout the world bring every resource at its
command against the sin of anti-Semitism.

Finally, Christians both in their private lives and in their
churches should take the lead in developing greater sympathy for those in need because of unequal opportunity,
those who are excluded by prevailing community customs
and sentiments, those who suffer persecution, anger and
despite because of their race.   They will seek to bring it
about that each racial group is judged by its best representatives and by the worthiest contributions it has made to the
life of humanity.   A conscious and constant effort should
be made to resist the fears and suspicions which tend to
arise from unlikeness and to cultivate friendship and cooperation in all undertakings that are of common concern
in the life of the community.   Here Christians must expect
to sacrifice popularity in loyalty to Christian insight and
love.

5. THE DIRECTION OF ADVANCE

Advance is possible, and a clear responsibility rests on
the church along two different lines — that of study and
that of immediate action.   There are problems in the relation of church and community on which further ecumenical thinking is necessary before effective Christian action
can be taken.   And there are certain concrete steps which
can be taken at once.

If the Christian conscience is to become a more effective
force in the weekday lives of Christians and hence of the
modern world, the church must attain a fuller insight into
the will of God for the common life today.   For this two

things are needed. One is a deeper understanding of the mind of God as revealed in Christ. The other is a more realistic understanding of the modern world. In the light of these, Christians must discover and formulate certain working principles on which they can agree as a common basis for Christian action and endeavor. Such " middle axioms " are intermediate between the ultimate basis of Christian action in community, " Thou shalt love thy neighbor as thyself " — which though for Christians un-assailable, is too general to give much concrete guidance for action — and the unguided intuition of the individual conscience. They are at best provisional and they are never unchallengeable or valid without exception or for all time, for it is in a changing world that God's will has to be ful-filled. Yet as interim principles they are indispensable for any kind of common policy.

But in most zones of the common life there are at this moment few such principles which are generally accepted by Christian people. Every day Christian individuals and groups are incurring responsibility for action or inaction on issues of the first magnitude, but there is no common mind among Christians by which they can be guided. But if our judgments are thus discordant it is largely because our thought and experience are still unduly partial and pro-vincial. The Oxford Conference and the preparation for it during the last three years have shown us something of what ecumenical discussion and study can do in promoting a deeper and truer and more really catholic apprehension. They have been only a beginning, however, and on many points we have only been able to clear the ground for such an advance by bringing out as clearly and trenchantly as possible the issues which at present divide us. The work thus begun must now be carried forward.

Among the problems calling for concerted investigation

by the best available Christian minds of all countries are the following:

(1) The Christian understanding of God's intention for the common life: How far the law of love which is to govern the inner lives and intimate personal relations of Christians apply also to their wider corporate relationships; what is the respective truth of the three main views described above, the views, namely, (a) that Christians should seek to bring all social life into conformity with the mind of Christ; (b) that they should regulate their corporate relationships by the natural morality of justice rather than directly by the supernatural morality of redemptive love; (c) that the sphere of these relationships is subject to no ideal standard but only to inner necessities arising out of the need of preserving human life from chaos.

(2) The problem of compromise for the Christian.

(3) The true significance of the claims of the " orders," especially *Volk* and nation and their relation to the claims of the universal church and the family of God.

(4) The nature of race; and in particular the question — partly scientific — of the desirability or unwisdom of intermixture of races.

IMMEDIATE STEPS: SOME PRACTICAL SUGGESTIONS

There is a call from God today

(1) To every local congregation, to realize in its own self at any cost that unity transcending all differences and barriers of class, social status, race and nation, which the Holy Spirit can and will create in those who are ready to be led by him.

(2) To the different churches in any district, to come together for local ecumenical witness in worship and work.

(3) To all Christians, to a more passionate and costly

concern for the outcast, the underprivileged, the persecuted, the despised in the community and beyond the community; just as Jesus himself was "moved with compassion" for the multitude and spent most of his life in ministering to their needs by healing and preaching. The recrudescence of pitiless cruelty, hatred and race discrimination in the modern world (including most notably anti-Semitism) is one of the major signs of its social disintegration. To these must be brought not only the weak rebuke of words but the powerful rebuke of deeds. Thus the unity of the church is advanced. For the church has been called into existence by God not for itself but for the world; and only by going out of itself in the work of Christ can it find unity in itself.

(4) To the church, to extend its concern to the particular areas of life where existing conditions in health, housing, employment and recreation in their distinctive rural and urban forms, as well as misunderstandings between old and young and tension between men and women, continually undo its work and thwart the will of God for his children. Thus the church should seek to express God's concern for every man in his own neighborhood and vocation.

(5) To the church, and particularly to the younger churches, to show a deeper interest in, and concern for, the rural community through whose labor and toil mankind is clothed and fed and which is in many parts of the world the most important unit of social life. The Christian church must learn from the strong non-Christian religions to take root in these little communities, conserving what is best in their traditional life but demonstrating a quality of communal living inspired by faith in Jesus Christ and by Christlike love that shall both judge and transform the existing social environment. From these may come exam-

ples of Christian group life and of a fellowship in common labor and worship which will be a priceless contribution to the common life of the world.

(6) To the church, to undertake new, prophetic and daring social experiments in local communities through which the general level of conscience may be raised.

(7) To the church, to play a healing and reconciling part in the conflicts, misunderstandings and hatreds which arise between interests or classes within the local community or nation.

(8) To those churches which have predominant influence in any country, to set their faces against any persecution of other churches or the raising of communal barriers to their free development.

(9) To the churches, to promote united study, fellowship and action; and in particular to arrange that successful experiments within various churches in finding new channels for the message of Christ to the people of this generation shall be made known in other churches also.

(10) To Christian men and women in the same vocation or industry, to meet together for prayerful discussion as to how, in their particular sphere of the common life, the practical problems which arise can be dealt with as God would require. Herein is a special responsibility of the laity.

(11) To members of the Christian church, to be ready to undertake responsibilities in local and national government. The church should seek to guide and support these its representatives in their efforts to solve the problems by which they are faced in the light of Christian principles.

(12) To all Christians, to seek by simplicity and discipline in personal living to go beyond the accepted standards of the community in the direction of the love revealed in Christ.

Finally, there is laid on the Christian churches in all

lands the obligation to create and to foster a solidarity and cooperation with one another that are stronger than all the divisions which now disrupt the family of mankind. The ecumenical movement which has found expression in the conference at Oxford should become an integral part of the life of every church, every local congregation, every individual Christian. To help to create it, to support it, to develop it, is a solemn responsibility to God, who so loved the world that he gave his only begotten Son for its sin. Thus shall be plainly manifested to mankind in its chaos and division something of that peace and order of brotherly love which come only from God and from Jesus Christ his Son, our Lord.

ADDITIONAL REPORT OF THE SECTION
ON CHURCH AND STATE *

1. THE PRESENT SITUATION

O NE OF THE outstanding facts in the present world situation is the increasing significance of the state in the total life of mankind. This shows itself not only in a great expansion of the area of its competence, but in a far-reaching
glorification and even religious exaltation of the state, its
symbols and its representatives. This situation can be
judged from many different standpoints, and as many different practical attitudes will result. Our specific standpoint is that of the Christian church.

Every attempt to understand the new tendencies in political life today will be mistaken if it ignores its close
relation to the comprehensive revolution through which
mankind is passing in the modern world.

(a) *Disintegration and Reintegration in the Modern
World*. Generally speaking, one can describe the situation
as a mixture of far-reaching disintegration and attempts at
totalitarian reintegration.

* This fuller report is based on the printed draft report issued in advance of the conference to its members. This draft report was fully discussed in the section and regarded as on the whole a satisfactory statement.
It was agreed by the section that in addition to the shorter report presented
to the conference there should also be a longer document based on the
original draft. The section instructed its officers to prepare this revised
draft of the memorandum in accordance with certain instructions given by
the section, and in the light of the discussions both in the section and in
the plenary session of the conference when the report was presented. Owing to the shortness of the time in which the task had to be undertaken,
the revision is less complete than had been intended, and the present report
is to a large extent the original report with a considerable number of
alterations and additions resulting from the discussions at Oxford.

Thinking men and women all over the world are increasingly coming to the conclusion that the present disintegration of inherited institutions and values and the birth pangs of new forms of human behavior and community life are not merely one of the usual, recurring cycles of depressions; they are a sign of a deep-seated change in the whole of human life. The World War and the period which followed it have revealed the breakup of Western civilization, a breakup the repercussions of which have affected other parts of the world and other civilizations. The industrialization and mechanization of life, as it has developed under the influence of the amazing progress of natural science during the last hundred years, not only betokens social progress but also gives rise to more doubtful consequences. The inherited social bonds and forms of community, which gave the individual standing ground and an organic connection with life, have been subjected in our time through excessive urbanization and active world trade to a continuous disruption. Morality and custom, which gave to the community a stable structure and to the individual security and a sense of direction derived from the legacy of wisdom bequeathed by his forefathers, have been widely undermined by new ideals and ways of thought. The growth of natural communities, in which man could be in the full sense of the term at home, has been restricted or destroyed by the chance agglomeration of isolated individuals into anonymous masses, in which dull resignation or revolutionary resentment is the prevailing temper.

But the dialectical character of the historical process is also recognizable today. It would give a one-sided picture if we were to emphasize only the aspect of disintegration. Powerful currents are flowing in the opposite direction and impelling toward new forms of community. The inborn longing of man for community and loyalty sets itself against the unchartered freedom and individualistic atomism of our day. These movements nonetheless are apt to fall into the other extreme. The efforts to find a way out of the intolerable strain and difficulty of the life of our day also tend, unconsciously or expressly, to deny the positive achievements of past generations. In many places the ideals of freedom, equality, self-determination and tolerance, and the newly awakened ideals of authority, obedience, sacrifice and surrender to the whole are regarded as mutually exclusive. Closely bound up with this attitude is the fact that the various forces which are seeking to check the process of widespread disintegration concentrate upon a particular section of life which is declared to be the center of a new order to the exclusion of all others. The class, the people, the state, or some other entity is given an absolute value. It demands and receives full surrender and unconditional loyalty.

The process of disintegration and reintegration is found in very different forms in individual countries and parts of the world, and is felt with varying degrees of intensity. The continent of Europe, which was the scene of the World War, has been most deeply affected. Other countries, in which the forms of the state taken over from the nineteenth century have suffered little change and where the breakdown of inherited forms of life has not affected the classes that have been politically and culturally in the ascendant, find themselves — or believe themselves to be — in a position of relative stability. But even here signs of an epochal change — social, political, moral — are recognizable.

(b) *Dechristianization of Society*. These violent changes in the whole cultural life are closely bound up with moral and spiritual changes, rooted far back in history, the results of which are becoming especially clear to our generation. We are confronted by the fact that great masses of men are gripped by an irreligious secularism which, after a period of preponderant indifference to the Christian faith, is taking an increasingly definite form and affecting an ever widening area of human life. Its relation to the Renaissance and the Enlightenment is well known. It was furthered by modern natural science in the confidence that all human problems were soluble by the constructive intellect and through material means. It should not be forgotten also that the necessity for concentrating all energies on the provision of a bare minimum for existence, which constituted the life of untold numbers of men, exhausted the spiritual and moral capacity of great masses. The securing of the outward means of life, the pursuit of individual and collective good fortune, were ruling ideals which also conditioned the ethical content of social life. The period after the World War showed in a terrible way that this secularism and practical materialism had only one more step to take to pass over into an aggressive and intolerant atheism bent on fashioning a new kind of man, not only in indifference but in conscious opposition to God.

A new element in this situation lies in the fact that this wave of secularism, which left a spiritual vacuum by destroying inherited religious symbols and ethical values, is accompanied by the irruption of new forms of faith and the rediscovery of old religions. The suppressed religious longing of secularized humanity is breaking through with elemental force and taking form in movements which inspire a passionate subordination to the collectivity. Men are following the many social and political symbols and banners with religious fervor because they promise them a unifying center for life and a new fellowship. Man, adrift from God, is making himself new idols because he cannot live without some object of adoration and sacrifice.

(c) *The Depreciation and the Glorification of Political*

Authority. The intensive struggle for political power is part and parcel of the confusing blend of contradictory purposes and mutually hostile forces which characterizes this period of extensive change. On the one hand, the process of secularization and increasing disintegration has invaded the sphere of the state, has robbed it of its religious glamor, and has made political authority merely a means in the competition between private and collective interests. The proclamation of an untrammelled individualism, the preponderance of economic aims, the unchecked exploitation of parliamentary institutions for the prosecution of group and class interests and of political liberties for revolutionary movements, are some of the factors which in many lands have helped to undermine political authority and have produced the danger of political impotence and universal anarchy. To a large extent respect for law and order has disappeared. Frequently the state, which ought to have been able to check this process of general disintegration, has not done so; indeed, sometimes it has even helped to accelerate it.

The swing of the pendulum has come with amazing rapidity. In some countries groups or parties, impelled by a passionate sense of " mission," have seized political power by means of revolution and have not lost a moment in consolidating and strengthening their position. The longing of the masses for a new order of life, whatever form it may assume, if only it promises to relieve the intolerable strain of their social and political condition, has given the impetus to this renewed belief in the state. Thus the new state — as a powerful body which supports and fulfills collective aspirations and as a helper in time of urgent need — is acclaimed with gratitude, homage and surrender. More and more powerfully the state is asserting and enforcing its claim on man. In many places, however, this new estimate of and actual increase in the power of the state goes much further. Just as in former times men were familiar with the ruler who claimed absolute homage or divine honors, so today the principle of personal rule and individual responsibility for the direction of the state has been reborn. World philosophies, old and new, provide the theoretical apparatus for this cult of the state and strengthen its emotional appeal. The state becomes the bearer of a myth.

(d) *The Emergence of Totalitarian Tendencies.* The dangerous character of this general intensification of the power of the state in both theory and practice is due to the fact that in many countries it is connected with a totalitarian claim. It is true, of course, that at earlier periods in history the state has sometimes extended its claim beyond the political and legal sphere into the sphere of personal and social life. The principle of sovereignty, which is essential to the modern state, is potentially totalitarian. In the age of absolutism and religious intolerance the state exercised its influence over wide spheres of personal and corporate life, and the democratic and liberal movements of the eighteenth and nineteenth centuries were essentially a reaction against this absolutism. The nineteenth and twentieth centuries, with their economic and social problems and the increased financial power of the state, came to believe more and more in the effectiveness of state regulation. Yet it was only during and after the World War that this tendency extended once more to the spiritual sphere, claiming the right to mold man as a whole. In a number of countries, where the disintegration of the community had reached an advanced stage, the total unification of community life, with the help of all the means of political power, was felt by many people to be the only way out of the threatened chaos.

It would, however, lead to a false judgment if we spoke

of totalitarian tendencies only in connection with certain countries. It is of the utmost importance to bear in mind that the totalitarian state is only the political expression of a tendency which can just as well take other forms and have other points of crystallization. Even in countries where the ruling ideas are those of liberalism and democracy, economic and political forces are at work which must lead to a rigid control of economic life, of public opinion, of national habits, and in general to a greater unification of the national being. Even where the state does not seek to influence men directly, but leaves wide room for the activities of religious and other formative societies, such tendencies are nonetheless noticeable. The steadily growing submission of citizens to public education and services, the unifying influence, often unconscious, which the ruling social group exerts over the whole of society, lead in fact to a uniformity of spirit and of behavior. The universal nature of totalitarianism becomes even more strikingly evident when we consider its close relation to war. The World War meant for the belligerent nations an experiment in the total unification of the functions of society on a scale hitherto almost unknown. So, too, anxiety about the next war and the military necessity of preparing the people over a long period of time for this terrible possibility are powerful incentives to totalitarian development.

(e) *The Relation of the State to the Church.* It is a sign of the times that the church situation of our own day is frequently compared with the pre-Constantine period. The reason for this comparison does not lie mainly in the fact that in certain countries the Christian church is being persecuted or threatened with suppression. It is justified chiefly because the Christian church is now confronted by masses of people who are alienated from her, either in a spirit of indifference or of active hostility.

After the freedom of the pre-Constantine period the church became in large degree dependent on the state and the groups which ruled it. It was only after the medieval state had been weakened by feudalism and the power of a state controlled by the will of a single ruler had been broken up into a variety of contractual relations between classes and corporations that a progressive emancipation of the church became possible. The fact that the church, as a result of the weakness of the state, itself gained temporal power and was thus able to confront the state on a footing of equality as an independent authority, endangered its own inmost nature. As soon as the modern state — in the fifteenth century — began to develop its sovereignty, it succeeded in reasserting its dominion over the church within its territory by means of the *jus reformandi*. The religious division following on the Reformation brought the churches into closer association with and dependence upon the state. Even after the ruling classes, as a result of the Enlightenment, had to some extent drifted away from the church the old close relation between church and state still existed. It was not until the nineteenth century that this bond was loosened, and the religious neutrality of the liberal state became an essential element in this process of secularization. It is true, of course, that at the present time in certain countries the attitude of the state is not only tolerant but in a varying degree also friendly, so that fruitful cooperation is still possible. But here too the increasing secularization of political life is bearing its fruit. A little noticed subordination of the church to the state is found in the fact that the church is seldom favored for its own sake, but only in so far as it is regarded as useful for the welfare of the state or as part of the historical inheritance of the nation. Thus modern states are severing themselves from Christian influence. Many have already gone a step further and have deprived the churches of those official rights formerly granted them by the state, thus placing the churches in an entirely new situation. Where an aggressive atheism is rampant within a state the repression of the church and a return to pre-Constantine conditions are inevitable.

(f) *The Need for Repentance and Reconsecration.* Such a diagnosis of the present life of the state does not give the church any reason to indulge in a pharisaical complacency. The church itself is involved in this whole situation. It is itself part and parcel of this lost world, with its absolutisms and its heresies, its inadequacy and its rebellion against God. The church is forced to recognize that the present situation, with all its suffering and its distress, with all its despairing attempts to create in its own strength a world apart from God, is a judgment upon itself. It must recognize, in the totalitarianism of the present day, an indictment of its own individualism and false spirituality. Its inward weakness and division, its lack of trust in the power of its Lord to conquer the evil in the heart of man in the world, its unreadiness to face the facts and the problems of a new period in history, have to a great extent prevented it from proclaiming the good news of the divine salvation with convincing authority. The church has taken too little trouble to show and to make visible in its own life the meaning of the fact that " the kingdom of God is among you."

2. THE CRUCIAL ISSUES BEFORE THE CHURCH

In the two thousand years of its history the church has known no escape from the struggle to achieve in the light of its own message a right attitude toward the problems and tasks with which the existence of the state confronts it. At every period the same problem presents itself anew. In our own time, in which perhaps to a greater extent than in any previous generation the traditional solutions and the experiences of the past have been thrown into the melting pot, it is more than ever necessary that the church should come to grips with this problem in all its range and complexity and not be content to concern itself merely with matters of secondary importance or with palliatives. There are three main groups of questions which in this field call for fundamental thought and responsible action in the coming years by Christian men and women throughout the world.

(a) *The Christian Sanction of the State.* The over-straining of political authority in the direction of absolutism and mythological idealization and its demand for unreserved loyalty and devotion, and equally on the other hand the opposing tendencies to minimize or even to deny the rights of the state, have raised with a new urgency the question of the sanction of political sovereignty. As soon as the church attempts to define its attitude toward particular questions of politics it is inevitably forced back on the ultimate question of the function of the state in God's providential ordering of human life.

(b) *The Responsibility of the Church to the State.* The functions of the state in modern social life are extremely comprehensive and many-sided. The state is not merely concerned with external security and the maintenance of internal order and justice. It takes both science and economics under its guardianship. It is actively interested in the education of the rising generation and in the religious and moral life of the people. By its decisions, by its fostering or its neglect of the manifold interests of society, it directs the whole in accordance with its will. While the Christian's loyalty to the state cannot imply an unreserved submission to its will and while in most civil matters considerable latitude is allowed for the exercise of personal responsibility, the question nevertheless arises for the conscience, Wherein lies the distinctive responsibility of the church and of its members in relation to the state in all its varied activities? What light does the Christian understanding of life shed on the wide field of political action and on the way in which its responsibilities may be fulfilled in obedience to the will of God?

(c) *The Christian View of Freedom and Authority.* The immense extension of the field of state activity and authority during the past century, and especially the powerful totalitarian tendencies in modern society since the World War, have given a new urgency to the question of the limits of political authority and of the freedom of personal, religious, cultural and other forms of activity within the common life. A Christian answer is needed to a double question — that of the freedom of the church and of its members to bear witness within the political order in word and deed to their Lord, and that of the freedom of men in general to live in accordance with the high responsibility of those who have been created in the image of God.

3. THE POSITION OF THE CHURCH

(1) The Christian Sanction of the State

(a) *The Church as the Starting Point.* The practical attitudes which Christians adopt toward the state and also their judgment concerning these attitudes reveal the widest diversity not only in regard to concrete matters but also in regard to fundamental questions of political life. These differences have their roots in the last resort in different convictions regarding the religious meaning of the state in the total context of life. The difference of starting point and approach is undoubtedly one of the principal causes of this disagreement. Sometimes Christians have taken individual statements in the Bible — for example, sayings in the Sermon on the Mount or utterances of St. Paul — as determining their political judgment and attitude. Sometimes they have allowed their actions and reactions to be governed by a particular affirmation of faith taken in isolation — for example, the kingdom of God, or the worth of human personality, or the unbridgeable opposition between the use of force and Christian love. At other times they have treated a contemporary solution of the relation between church and state which is valid for a particular historical epoch as being normative for all times, and have employed it as a standard for the solution of the problems of their own age.

It is not surprising, therefore, that the conceptions of the distinctively Christian understanding of political issues reveal a wide diversity in Christian thought today. Many Christians, for example, are convinced that the church is the only true interpreter of the divine law implanted in the essential nature of things, and consequently is entitled to speak the authoritative word not only in regard to the motives which determine men's attitude in the political order but also regarding the purpose and nature of the state. Similarly others find in the witness of the Bible as a whole not only standards for the exercise of Christian responsibility in politics but also a deeper insight into the constitutive elements of political life than the ordinary reason or political experience can give. Others again believe that the Christian message does not include any new understanding of the meaning of the state, but only provides divine guidance for the personal attitude of the Christian within the political order.

All these differences, however, converge at an important point — i.e., the existence of the church. It is one of the most cheering and promising signs of our times that Christians all over the world have a growing consciousness of what the church of Jesus Christ in its distinctive being and fullness signifies as a living reality in the midst of this world. The more it is realized that the church is the great sustaining reality of life, the more will individual Christians and groups reach accord in their endeavors to bring political life under the sovereignty of Christ. The church of Christ as the community in which grace and love are at work in the totality of its life and witness must be our common standing ground. It is true that the affirmation of this truth will not automatically remove all our differences and difficulties, since the deepest divergences manifest themselves precisely in our understanding of the church. They will, however, be seen in a new perspective and find a common orientation.

(b) *The Contemporary State.* Political realities, political and legal theories, and ethical valuations, all in the most varied combinations, help to determine the understanding of the state. It is important to emphasize this fact here because many differences in the Christian attitude thereby become intelligible. Not only does Christian and theological thought influence political thought and political attitudes, but there is also a reverse influence. Of two Christians who hold the same form of Christian belief, the one as the result of his political experience may view the state primarily as a form of organic community providing for its order and advancement, while the other may see it above all as a harsh instrument of force, and thus the two must inevitably arrive at different judgments regarding the concrete questions of political conduct. The historical situation in which political action takes place must also be taken into account.

The word " state " is not everywhere used in the same sense. While in some countries it focuses the attention primarily on the agents of political life — namely, the people and government — in other areas the state is seen primarily as a community of law, the organs of which with their different responsibilities hold only a secondary place. In both cases, however, the same reality of social life is intended, and here also the conception is used in this sense and not as a philosophical abstraction. Not only in the long course of history but also in the contemporary situation the state appears in the most diverse forms and stages of development. Nonetheless it has one universal and decisive mark. Everywhere in recent centuries political power has consolidated itself in the name of sovereignty, whether this is exercised by parliaments, by dictators, or by parties, and it has established its complete independence over against other social powers and over against the church. The state, whether it is organized as a democracy or parliament or dictatorship, claims itself to determine and to make obligatory on all its subjects the extent of its competence and in what constitutional forms it will exercise it. It is true that there are states — for example, federal states — in which the political power is in a peculiar way distributed among different political entities. But even here there is a hierarchy of authority. The decisive matter is that every man is always and everywhere incorporated in a political order, or state, which assigns to him rights and duties, and from which he cannot escape so long as he remains within its sphere of power. Even the states which allow their citizens to participate in the framing of the laws and accord them much personal liberty, claim the right to determine with absolute freedom the extent of these rights and liberties through the recognized constitutional organ. And this claim, even in states which desire to be regarded as Christian, does not stop short at the church or freedom of worship or freedom of conscience.

The state, under the influence of political doctrines which go back directly or indirectly to the ancient theory of the state, is regarded as a social organism, as the indispensable and beneficial means of human coordination. The more recent political theories of political or social contract derive the state from the will of the people, which in it acquires a legal form, and have powerfully influenced political thought up to the present time. This view however is not undisputed. It is urged against it that the state essentially means a domination of one over others even when externally its constitution presents a different appearance. Whether it is true or not in particular historical situations, it is a fact that the state always tends, at least to a certain extent, to promote as the impartial bearer of power the interests of the whole, since this is the presupposition of the stability and endurance of every form of rule.

The state, and in a special sense the modern state, cannot be understood unless account is taken of the element of power. Externally the state is limited only by the power of other states and by international law, which, however, is not assured by any superior collective authority and which assumes before all else the independence of each state. Internally the supreme will of the state is limited only by the forms which the constitution provides for the formation of the political will. Unrestricted in the determination of its aims, the state possesses a monopoly of force and of the means of exercising it. The state plays therefore in the social existence of man a peculiar and predominant role, and since all power in the state rests in the last resort in the hands of men this fullness of power can be experienced not only by the ruling parties and by leaders of the state, but also by whole peoples. In this power lies not only the possibility of fulfilling the necessary tasks of the state on behalf of its people and on behalf of humanity, but also the great temptation to overstrain and abuse it. It is only the church that in the last resort can show the state the limit of its power.

(c) *The Christian Sanction of the State.* Throughout the centuries the Christian conscience has continually insisted that, whatever view may be taken of the political order, it is not a sphere of action unrelated to God. It has held firmly to the witness of the Bible that God is at work even in political life. It has regarded the paradoxical attitude of the early Christians as in accordance with reality. On the one hand the New Testament regards the state as a divine institution which has a definite part to play in the divine plan of salvation. On the other hand it points to diabolical forces at work in the political sphere. These affirmations of faith that the exercise of the political function is a manifestation of the divine will, and that it is nonetheless constantly being perverted and misused, are fundamental for our view of politics and have important consequences. The state has a divine sanction. Its authority and its dignity are based upon this fact. But it is not an end in itself nor a final end. It exists to serve the purposes of God. Thus all political action is confronted by the inevitable alternative, whether it is to be an instrument of or an obstacle to the gracious rule of God.

When, however, we try to develop this fundamentally Christian view of the state in greater detail we find differences of opinion. Many Christians regard the state as an expression of the divine law which penetrates the universe as a whole. The state is an order based upon the need of men for social life and serves the purpose of insuring order, peace and temporal welfare for the community. The divine law in the nature of things is both the origin and the criterion of all political life. It is an ideal which lays practical obligations upon mankind. But only in the church does the higher meaning of the state become evident. The state is a temporal means for guiding man toward his supernatural end.

Another view also derives the authority of the state from the divine moral world order. The moral obligations which are written in the conscience of all men are to be realized in the state. The state serves the divine purpose by realizing the ideals of humanity — freedom, equality and universal well-being — and by guaranteeing to all men the most favorable external conditions for their free self-development.

A third view lays special emphasis upon the connection between the state and the nation and regards the nation as the preeminent form of social life, established by God himself. In this view the nation is conceived as the social form of human life which transcends all others. The state is the organization of the national community and the agent by which its historical mission is achieved. Since by its sovereignty it protects and furthers the undisturbed development of the national character, it must be recognized by the Christian church as an instrument of the divine will manifested in history.

A fourth view lays the main stress on the element of coercion in the state, and on the radical disintegration which continually threatens the community through the presence of human sinfulness and social evil. The state is regarded as a dike to keep out the floods of chaos, as a harsh and indispensable instrument of the divine will which makes possible a relatively peaceful and humane life. It belongs to the paradoxical nature of the state that in its exercise of force it seems to be absolutely opposed to the Christian virtues of love, humility and gentleness, and yet that it must be accepted as a well fitted instrument of the sovereign will of God for the prevention of disaster. The authority and legal order of the state are the one fixed point on which in the fallen world the whole social order depends.

(2) The Responsibility of the Church toward the State

(a) *Christian Loyalty to the State.* The responsibility of the church and of its members toward the state is grounded in its obedience to God. The attitude of Christians to the actual states in which they live will in consequence have a double character. It will be positive and at the same time critical. It is a Christian duty to cooperate in the shaping of the political order through prayer, obedience and active participation. But both unqualified submission to the prescriptions of the authorities and a passive indifference to political issues are irreconcilable with the conviction that God is the unconditional Lord of this sphere of human life. Members of the church are the apostles of a righteous and loving God, and they must take the lead in courageous criticism, in the realistic testing of political ideals and methods by their contribution to the common good, and in an unceasing struggle for a fuller realization of the demands of justice and love both in legislation and in administration, both in local and in national government. If individual Christians or groups are compelled for the sake of conscience and after consultation with their fellow Christians to disobey measures taken by the state, the church, whether national or supra-national, should stand by them and thereby show the solidarity of the community of faith. Where circumstances permit it should make representations to the state with a view to a removal of the difficulties. A controversial question which has again become acute in many parts of the world and calls for earnest attention is the question at what points disobedience to the commands of the state becomes a Christian duty and by what means it should find expression —

e.g., how far the use of political pressure or even of revolutionary methods, in distinction from passive resistance, is legitimate for the attainment of social ends which appear from the Christian standpoint to be necessary.

The church has thus a direct and positive responsibility for the state and for its proper functioning. In this connection three large groups of questions make a special appeal to the Christian conscience. These are the Christian concern for the maintenance of law and justice, the exercise of force in the political sphere, and the task of the state in the cultural life of the community.

(b) *The Christian Concern for the Maintenance of Law and Justice.* The exercise of political power is, in the Christian view, not an end in itself. It is subordinate to the claim of God to be sovereign Lord and is to be used for his purposes. The message of the Old and New Testaments as well as the message of the church throughout the centuries expresses this conviction by saying that justice is the directive and limiting norm of all political conduct. In political strife, where one claim is opposed by another, what matters finally is the justice of God and his claim. This fundamental conviction leads to far-reaching conclusions. It relegates all political and social conflict to a secondary plane and removes its sting, since it commits the result to the hidden decision of God. It is at the same time a powerful incentive to the struggle for greater justice in all spheres of life.

For many Christians, justice as a political norm consists in giving to every man his due in his actual situation and his actual need. The principle of *suum cuique* and the norms of natural law which can be derived from it are regarded as the standard for the legal order of the community both in the relation of the citizens to one another and also in the relation between the state and its citizens. These principles of natural law, which struggle for realization in the legal organization of the community, are derived from the divine law which inspires and holds together the whole order of the universe.   Justice, therefore, can never mean the mere affirmation of existing social and economic conditions.   In the dynamic course of history the eternal order of the divine justice is ever struggling for fresh expression. Therefore the maintenance of law and order means an unceasing adjustment to the eternal order of law, and this in turn means a constantly renewed adjustment of the various social rights and duties for the sake of the common good.

Other Christians, however, would deny that this attempt to interpret justice in terms of the *suum cuique* throws any light upon the specifically Christian conception of law and order.   Rather, they would say, we must seek the criteria for Christian judgment and action in political matters in the revealed will of God.   Some find decisive standards in the precepts and statements of the Bible, above all in the Ten Commandments.   Others lay more emphasis upon the paradoxical and, indeed, antithetical relation between the principle of justice and that self-sacrificing love which Christ has revealed in his life and death as the will of God. They regard the law — as a definite way of ordering the relation between individuals and groups in the community — primarily as a barrier against human caprice and arrogance.   The system of law, moreover, inasmuch as it defines and limits the spheres of power in relation to one another and gives to the institutions of the community stability, constancy, the power of planning for the future, and security, is a protection from the danger of anarchy.   Finally, the critical principle of justice, which is ever at work within the law, is a force continually making for improvement. But even justice is not the highest end of political life but always something that falls short of the highest.   It is always pointing in hidden ways to something it cannot itself achieve, namely, that fellowship of divine love where there is no adjustment of rights and claims, because surrender and mutual service are regarded as the supreme law. But this does not mean that the legal order is superfluous for the Christian. Since he is still a sinner he needs it as a help and as a restraint. The sovereignty of Christ in and through his church transcends, it is true, all earthly legal orders, but at the same time it penetrates into them with its sanctifying and transforming influence. Hence the hidden meaning of the order of law is fulfilled only where the many difficult tasks and responsibilities of political life are subordinated to the command of the living and holy God, since " love is the fulfillment of the law."

(c) *The Place of Force in the Political Sphere.* The most difficult problem for the Christian conscience in political life is the use of force as a means of asserting the political will to power against all opposition. This conflict between Christian love and the use of force reaches its tragic climax in war. The great expansion of the activity of the state and the consequent dependence of men, both in their personal life and in their economic existence, on political factors, combined with the methods of influencing the masses provided by modern technique, have made it possible for the state to subject its citizens in a new way not only to physical pressure but also to moral and spiritual pressure. All these new developments make it necessary that fresh thought be given to the traditional doctrine of the " sword " of the state and to the question of the legitimacy and limits of the use of force.

The necessity for the use of force, however difficult and morally questionable it may be, must be admitted in principle, since without it the state would not be able to maintain the system of law and order which it protects. But there is much well grounded difference of opinion on the question whether certain kinds of force are under all circumstances forbidden to the Christian, and at what point in concrete instances the line should be drawn. These differences come out particularly clearly in opinions about war. But in spite of these differences there is a settled Christian conviction that the use of force, however unavoidable it may be for the fulfillment of the distinctive tasks of the state, is in itself absolutely opposed to the love commandment and that it can be used only in the certainty of divine forgiveness. It is therefore part of the political responsibility of the community to watch the ends for which the state uses its power and also to see that the use of force is reduced to a minimum. Further, it should be insisted that the exercise of force, apart from exceptional instances of extreme emergency, should take place within the framework of generally accepted law and should remain the exclusive monopoly of the organs of the state, in order that it may not become the instrument either of caprice or of the private and collective lust of power.

(d) *The Function of the State in the Cultural Life of the Community*. Another question which has become increasingly urgent in the modern state is that of the responsibility of the state for the cultural life of the community, in the widest sense of the word. Control by the state of culture and national morality is no new phenomenon. The ancient " *polis* " is a typical example of this view of the state. On the contrary, it may be maintained that the partial release of these spheres from state control within the liberal state represents something new in political history. It is in any case an incontestable fact that the contemporary state is not content merely to protect the varied life of the community by means of its political and legal organization, but claims the right to direct the mind and heart of the nation along definite lines. The extent to which this takes place, of course, varies greatly.

The claim of the state to control the cultural life and to monopolize popular education, public opinion and the character training of its citizens creates a serious issue for the church. The situation which it has to meet is that the state may develop into a secularized church with a world view of its own. The problem is one of the first urgency, to which Christian thought must be directed with far greater energy than has yet been shown.

(3) The Christian View of Freedom and Authority

(a) *The Nature of the Problem*. The modern growth of non-Christian forms of totalitarianism, whether these find their center in class or race or nation or in some other special segment of life, has brought strongly into the foreground the question of sovereignty and freedom and the limits of political control. The point at which the church comes into immediate conflict with the totalitarian tendencies of the state is where these tendencies are inspired by a myth and a religious or pseudo-religious claim on the unconditional devotion of men — in other words, where these tendencies attempt to be a substitute for the church. In many countries the attempt is being made by direct political pressure or by the pressure of public opinion or by other more subtle methods to inoculate the church with the ruling ideology. Elsewhere also there is found a tendency through the use of political measures to curtail the freedom of the church at one point or another and to impose on it fetters which restrict the free carrying out of its mission. The church has in these circumstances an immediate interest in the limitation of the state's authority in order that it may be free to carry out its special task.

This development in the direction of an extension of

political influence and authority may be observed also in other spheres. The relation of the state and freedom has today become a burning question in regard to the family, science, public morals, and philosophical outlook. With growing insistence, therefore, the question is addressed to the church of its witness and action when human personality is denied, when truth and right are subordinated to utilitarian ends, or when the state arbitrarily, by physical or moral pressure, deprives men of their own independent life. It is indispensable that the church clarify its mind in respect to the grounds on which it regards human freedom in general even over against the state as a special concern of its own, and in regard to the measures which it ought to take to conserve this freedom. What is at stake is the Christian understanding of man. It is on this point that the Christian teaching regarding the worth and freedom of man has a decisive importance, since to a large extent it must determine the attitude of the church toward all political measures which do not directly touch the exercise of its own functions.

(b) *The Freedom of the Church in its Different Functions.* In thinking of the church, more particularly in relation to the state, we tend under the influence of earlier habits of thought to think in the first instance of the contrast between a state church and a free church. We think, that is to say, of the organic and legal connection between church and state and of the degree of state supervision of the churches. This tendency in thinking was natural so long as the state acknowledged the fact of the church and of the Christian faith, but when the state as a result of secularization adopted more and more a neutral or aloof attitude toward Christianity and the churches, or rejected the Christian faith altogether, or attempted to subordinate it to its own aims and world view, questions of *jura in sacra* and *jura circa sacra* became of secondary importance. Here we are concerned primarily with the freedom of the church which is necessary for its own existence, quite apart from the question whether the church is organically connected with the state or is a free organization legally recognized or tolerated by the state.

The church as the messenger of the gospel and as the community in which freedom in God is a living reality represents the ultimate boundary against totalitarian tendencies of every kind. The existence of the church is a barrier to every attempt to build a common life on a purely secular basis. The church is free in so far as it is true to its Lord, and it must maintain this freedom against all the claims and temptations of the world. Hence the freedom of the church cannot be given from the outside by the state. The most the state can do is to give the church legal protection. When it gives this the church will gratefully accept it as a conscious or unconscious tribute of the political authorities to the sovereignty of its Lord. But when the church's freedom is restricted the conflict between church and state becomes acute. For the church demands freedom to proclaim the gospel to all mankind and in all spheres of life, not for its own sake but because it has received this commission from God, who is also Lord of the state.

This freedom of the church, which it must in case of necessity defend against the encroachment of the state, includes all the functions which are necessary for carrying out its own commission. It is this public character of the church which makes the whole problem so difficult. Secret communion with God in prayer and worship cannot be attacked by the state, but the public proclamation of the gospel and its application to the whole sphere of Christian life can be restricted and hindered by the state in various ways.

First in importance comes the public proclamation of the Christian message. Since this message lays bare the self-assertion of the world and its denial of its Creator, and proclaims the new salvation wrought by God in Christ, it is directed to mankind as a whole. Hence the church cannot refrain from using all available methods of public communication such as speech, print, the press and the radio. This freedom includes as a matter of course opportunities for common worship and of association for church purposes apart from periods of ordinary public worship. The conduct of foreign missions must also be included among the fundamental functions of the church.

Under modern conditions, in which the secularized community is emancipating itself from Christian influence in its motives and standards, it is of decisive importance for the future of the church that it should be allowed to bring up and educate its own members in the spirit of Christianity.

The freedom which the church must claim includes also its service of love to those who are in need, to the sick, and to the oppressed. It must include further the opportunity of cooperation through its members in the transformation of the social order in the light of the divine will.

The religious discharge of this task presupposes that the church is able to regulate its external forms of church order and administration according to its own principles, whether with or without the understanding and support of the state authorities. This requirement is of special importance for the existence of ecclesiastical minorities, since they are most readily exposed to the danger of interference in their life by the state or by a church representing the majority or by a particular ecclesiastical group through the exercise of political pressure.

(c) *The Christian Interest in Human Freedom in Gen-*

eral. In regard to the responsibility of the church for the maintenance of human freedom, its extent and the means and ways of its realizations, there exists considerable disagreement among Christians. Attention may be briefly directed to three conceptions which have their roots in profound theological differences.

For many Christians the unhindered self-development of the personality is the starting point of their thought about these questions. The state exists for the sake of the free man. The independence of the individual person and his freedom to fulfill himself in accordance with the immanent laws of his being is the decisive limit of the state. Since, according to this view, personal individuality is the highest good in history, every political and legal measure which infringes on the personal life is unjustified. It is plainly one of the primary responsibilities of the church to further this unhindered freedom of every man and to protect it against attacks from the side of the state, since it is the gospel itself that proclaims with indisputable clearness the infinite worth of the individual soul. The church must therefore demand freedom in the political sphere for the human person, for the family, for economic activity, and for the various cultural and other associations.

Other Christians would maintain a precisely opposite point of view — namely, that there are no specifically Christian grounds and standards for the limitation of the state so long as the essential tasks of the church itself are not involved. Christian freedom is an inner or eschatological freedom for which it is irrelevant how far the state extends its claims in the sphere of the social life. The freedom of the natural man and his subordination to the commands of the state is a matter of political responsibility. How far, for example, the state controls and guides economic effort and how in its legislation it regulates the position of national and racial minorities are matters that belong to the sphere of political expediency. The church has no authority to demand in the name of the gospel any rights either for individuals or for human associations. That is not to say that the state has an unlimited competence. The limits of its authority, however, have to be decided not from the standpoint of the gospel or of the claims of the individual, but from that of the responsibility of the state to order and protect the common life. Without presuming to interfere in the province of political authority the church must make it its concern to care for the oppressed and persecuted in compassionate love.

The majority of Christians, however, with whatever differences in detail, would regard a third conception as more in harmony with the nature of the gospel. They would neither agree with the view that the freedom of the church is nothing more than a special instance of human freedom in general, nor with the view that it is not the business of the church to take part after its own fashion in the unending struggle for a just equilibrium between political sovereignty and human freedom. The church has indeed no interest in the unrestricted expression of all possible forms of human activity. It knows the demonic impulses which belong to fallen man and which constantly transform freedom into license, and consequently when the state fails through weakness to protect one against the arbitrary conduct of another it must be a matter of serious concern for the church. On the other hand, the church knows that man has been created in the image of God and has therefore an indestructible value, which the state must not impair but rather safeguard. The destiny of man and the different social activities in their proper functioning — such as marriage, the family, the nation, and culture — constitute an irremovable limit of the state which it cannot with impunity transgress. A state which destroys human personality or human associations, or subordinates them to its own ends, is therefore incompatible with the Christian understanding of life. The state ought, on the contrary, to employ its resources to insure that human freedom should find growing expression in the service of the neighbor and should not be used according to the prompting of natural inclination for self-assertion and irresponsible behavior. In this task it cannot dispense with the cooperation of the church. It is therefore in no sense an attempt to meddle with what does not belong to it, but a simple act of obedience to God who is righteous and loving when the church, so far as circumstances allow it, becomes the champion of true human freedom in co-operation with the state and when necessary in criticism of its measures.

4. PRESENT TASKS AND DUTIES

(a) *Faith as the Motive for Christian Political Activity.* From this survey of the principles which determine the Christian attitude toward the state we turn in conclusion to a brief consideration of the present tasks which follow from them.

This first of all, that it is the duty of the church, both when acting in its representative capacity and in its relation to its individual members, to bring to all that is done and planned the dynamic of Christian faith. What we need to emphasize most of all at the present time is the fact that the primary defect of church and state alike, so far as political activity is concerned, is not the lack of a program of action but the decline of faith and the lack of selfless love. Since God is Lord of the state the one thing that matters is that men should have living communion with God and trust and obey him unreservedly. The more the Christian community receives from God strength, confidence, courage, joy, and liberty, the more will the powers of the eternal world radiate from it into the world. Precisely because its strength is derived from the supra-political sphere will its influence be felt spontaneously and effectively in the political sphere. The more clearly the church proclaims that Christ has conquered all the principalities and powers of this world, and that it is his will to be victorious in the life of every man and woman, the more will the church help the world. And this in two ways: first of all, it will make it easier for each generation to deal with its own political problems as they occur; second, the political sphere as a whole will be seen in a new and supra-mundane light, and when thus reduced to its proper level the atmosphere of politics will be sweetened and purified. If politics is to be redeemed we need renewed men and women. Hence it is the first and central political task of the church to pray the Father of our Lord Jesus Christ to create in all its members a living faith in himself. The community which comes into being through the Word and the sacraments, and which consists of missionary groups living in Christian fellowship, will be a community in which — in spite of all the sinfulness and imperfection of Christians — the life lived in God will become visible to the world. Only when this happens can we have Christian politics in any true sense of the word.

(b) *Special Duties Incumbent upon the Churches Today*. From this primary duty certain derived duties follow, as for example:

(1) That the churches should summon their own members to repentance, both as individuals and organized bodies, for their sins of omission and of commission, and should pray for the spirit of consecration which shall make of them both in their separate and in their united activities agents which God may use for his purpose in the world.

(2) That they should bring into existence within the local community, the nation and the world such agencies of cooperative action as shall make it possible for them to discharge effectively such tasks as can be done in common.

(3) That they should summon their individual members in their several callings, not only their clerical but also their lay members, men and women, to cooperate with the state in such constructive tasks as may be for the good of the whole.

(4) That they should guard for all churches, both as groups of witnessing Christians and in their organized capacity, the opportunity of worship, of witness, of service and of education, which is essential to their mission, and this not for their own sake only but for the sake of the states.

In order to discharge these tasks aright the churches need to develop further their agencies of cooperative study in order that the work begun at Stockholm and Oxford may be carried to effective completion. If they are to deal with the political situation of the present day in the Christian spirit it will not be enough for them merely to follow well trodden paths with greater earnestness and fervor. Rather will they be challenged to reconsider and re-examine the presuppositions, standards and methods which they have employed in the past. The chief purpose of this self-examination will be to enable them to distinguish more clearly than they have hitherto done their own distinctive function and to bring to the discharge of that function all the help that can come to them through cooperative study in the light of modern knowledge.

(c) *The Responsibility of the Church as a Whole for the Freedom of Its Members.* In addition to the special duties affecting its own members and the state with which it has more immediate connection each church has a further duty as a member of the church universal. This is to follow with sympathetic interest the fortunes of those, Christians and non-Christians, who are victims of cruelty and oppression, and to do what it can to secure for them a treatment compatible with the dignity of their human personality as children of God.

Wherever any church is being persecuted or its public work and influence are being hindered by the power of the state, we ought to remember that church with loving intercession and active sympathy.   Even in countries where a positive attitude toward Christianity is expressed in the official recognition of a state church there are tendencies at work which limit Christian freedom against which we need to be on our guard.   Such threats to Christian liberty, whether overt or implied, lay upon ecumenical Christianity a responsibility of the most serious character.   The church in its ecumenical capacity cannot remain indifferent while in various countries, either with the active cooperation or the silent approval of the political authorities, the service of the church is made difficult or almost impossible.   What the churches which still enjoy freedom can do to help any sister church thus deprived of liberty of Christian witness, they should do.

It goes without saying that in protesting against persecution on the part of the state the church itself must renounce all forms of persecution, whether by Christians against other Christians or by Christians against adherents of other religions.   Only as in addition to vindicating its own freedom it becomes spokesman for the freedom of man as man will it be in a position to fulfill its God-given task. In this struggle for a larger and fuller life we are not concerned that the church should claim rights for itself or even that it should seek to secure its own stability.   The one thing that matters is that it should be free to proclaim the good news of Christ, without let or hindrance, in accordance with the commission given to the church by its Lord (Matt. 28:18–20) .